T0270189

# THE BRIDGE

OTHER BOOKS BY KEITH MAILLARD

# THE

# BRIDGE

*Writing Across the Binary*

## KEITH MAILLARD

© KEITH MAILLARD 2021

All rights reserved. No part of this publication may be reproduced, stored in a retrieval system, or transmitted in any form or by any means, graphic, electronic, or mechanical — including photocopying, recording, taping, or through the use of information storage and retrieval systems.— without prior written permission of the publisher or, in the case of photocopying or other reprographic copying, a licence from the Canadian Copyright Licensing Agency (Access Copyright), One Yonge Street, Suite 800, Toronto, Ontario, Canada, M5E 1E5.

Freehand Books acknowledges the financial support for its publishing program provided by the Canada Council for the Arts and the Alberta Media Fund, and by the Government of Canada through the Canada Book Fund.

 Canada Council for the Arts  Conseil des Arts du Canada  Alberta Government  Canada

Freehand Books
515 – 815 1st Street SW   Calgary, Alberta   T2P 1N3
www.freehand-books.com

Book orders: UTP Distribution
5201 Dufferin Street   Toronto, Ontario   M3H 5T8
Telephone: 1-800-565-9523   Fax: 1-800-221-9985
utpbooks@utpress.utoronto.ca   utpdistribution.com

Library and Archives Canada Cataloguing in Publication
Title: The bridge : writing across the binary / Keith Maillard.
Names: Maillard, Keith, 1942– author.
Identifiers: Canadiana (print) 20200372181 | Canadiana (ebook) 2020037222X
| ISBN 9781988298788 (softcover) | ISBN 9781988298795 (EPUB) | ISBN
9781988298801 (PDF)
Subjects: LCSH: Maillard, Keith, 1942– | LCSH: Gender-nonconforming
people — West Virginia — Biography. | LCSH: Gender nonconformity. |
CSH: Authors, Canadian (English) — 20th century — Biography. | LCGFT:
Autobiographies.
Classification: LCC PS8576.A49 Z46 2021 | DDC C818/.5403—dc23

Edited by Deborah Willis
Book design by Natalie Olsen, Kisscut Design
Cover photo © 2Dew/Shutterstock.com
Author photo by Mary Maillard
Printed on FSC® certified paper and bound in Canada by Marquis

Chapters 1 and 3 of "The Movement" include some writing that originally appeared in "The Author's Afterward" to Looking Good. Copyright © 2006 by Keith Maillard from Looking Good. Reprinted with permission of Brindle & Glass, an imprint of TouchWood Editions.

MIX
Paper from responsible sources
FSC
www.fsc.org   FSC® C103567

*for Mary*

And in a world where femininity is so regularly dismissed, perhaps no form of gendered expression is considered more artificial and more suspect than male and transgender expressions of femininity. —JULIA SERANO

There is nothing in human nature or the requirements of human social organization which intrinsically requires that a culture be contradictory, repressive and productive of violent and frustrated personalities. —GARY SNYDER

If I can't describe who I am in this world — I am who I am, whether or not I can describe it — then I can't seek out others like me. —ANDREA BENNETT

# CONTENTS

# PROLOGUE

IN MARCH OF 1997 a lawyer in California called to tell
me that my father had just died. I was deeply shaken.
My parents had split up when I was about a year old,
and I knew next to nothing about Gene Maillard, the
man who'd given me half my DNA. Except for a short
bitter speech that she always repeated word for word,
my mother had refused to talk about him. As an adult,
I'd made two attempts to find him, but I hadn't succeeded. He had died a wealthy man, a millionaire, and
he'd known who I was and where I was, but rather than
reaching out to me, he had named me in his will so he
could disinherit me. I was hurt and angry. My father's
executor, a kind man, sent me a few of my father's personal items including two large scrapbooks in which he
had documented his life. Okay, I thought, Gene might
not have left me any of his money, but he had left me his
story. I decided to write a book about him.

My father's absence might have had a huge impact on my life, but if it did, I wasn't sure how. How do you write about something you didn't have? The light in our basement guest room is a murky half-light, and sounds are muffled. I went down there, stretched out flat on the bed with a blanket over me, and talked into a digital recorder. I knew that what I was trying to do was impossible — to recover my child's mind — but I wanted to see how close I could get. I said whatever came to me and did not censor anything. When I finished each day, I jacked the recorder into my computer and watched my speech-recognition software transform my spoken words into text. I thought I'd do this for a day or two and that would be the end of it, but the memories kept coming for weeks. Much of what I was remembering had nothing to do with my father.

I gave the book I was writing a title, *Fatherless*, and I kept adding to it until it swelled up into a monstrosity — a huge, complicated, incoherent, hairy, seven-headed beast, the despair of its author, over a thousand pages. It's difficult to see your writing clearly when you're tangled up in it, so I set that impossible manuscript aside and worked on other things. When I came back to it, I saw what the problem was. It wasn't one book; there were at least two books in there. I created a file called *The Second Book*, and anything that was not about my father I dumped into that file. I went through *Fatherless* a number of times, becoming more ruthless with every pass, until I was satisfied that I had stripped away every bit of excess.

14

Eventually I had what I wanted — a focused narrative that was the story of my search for Gene Maillard and an account of his life. *Fatherless* was published by West Virginia University Press in the fall of 2019.

For a long time I didn't bother to look into the second file. I knew roughly what was in there — everything I had rejected — but if there was actually another book, I didn't know what it was. Much of what I had dumped into that file was about me as a child. I had suffered from "gender trouble" — to borrow Judith Butler's evocative term — so I decided to focus on that, but when I began working my way through the file, I discovered that gender issues were so intertwined with the story of my beginnings as a writer that I couldn't separate those two strands. Okay, so the gender-troubled little boy who would grow up to be a writer — that could be the heart of the matter — and what if I cut everything else? It took a while. I stripped away extended evocations of our neighborhood just after the war, biographies of family pets, West Virginia tall tales, accounts of Ohio River floods, family legends going back five generations, portraits of aunts and uncles and cousins, a ghost story or two, a comprehensive catalogue of everything I'd read up to the age of eighteen, and random musings about god knows what — all stuff that might be of interest to my daughters or a future biographer but probably to no one else. What was left was the beginning of this book.

*part 1*

# LIKE A GIRL

## 1

THE NOTION OF "GENDER IDENTITY" has been around since the 1950s and has largely been accepted by psychologists; it refers to the deep inner conviction we have about what gender we are. Most people know their gender identity by the time they are two or three. My memories don't go back quite that far, but as far back as I do remember, I was never certain. I asked my mother and grandmother over and over again, "Am I a boy, or am I a girl?" — asked so many times they got sick of answering and started getting mad at me, and then I would hear, "I *told you!*" They always told me that I was a boy, but I was never convinced. It would take me over sixty years to arrive at a clear understanding of my problem — I was trapped inside what we now would call "the gender binary," the notion that there are only two choices.

Not having a father seemed so ordinary that I didn't even think about it until I got old enough to play with other kids and found out that they all seemed to have fathers. Then I would say what my mother had taught me to say — "My parents are divorced." For a long time I didn't know what "divorced" meant.

I knew that my father's name was Eugene Charles Maillard. My mother didn't like to talk about him. She would only say a few things, and she always said those same few things in the exact same words. "He was a good dancer and lots of fun. He was the cheapest man who ever lived. He came from Canada, and the men in his family were glassblowers. He was French from Alsace-Lorraine, and he spoke French. He wanted you to be named after him. If you had been, you would have been the fourth Eugene Charles."

She would often ask me, "Aren't you glad you're not named Gene?" and I would always say, "Yes," and I *was* glad. I had a girl cousin named Jean so I thought Gene was a girl's name, and I didn't want to have a girl's name unless I *was* a girl. Because I didn't know for sure if I was a boy or a girl — but everybody said I was a boy — having a girl's name would have just made things worse.

"I told your father that everybody deserves their own name," my mother said. "*You* deserved your own name.

Gene was out of town when you were born. He called me up in the hospital, asked, 'How's Eugene?' and I said, 'His name's Keith,' and he hung up on me."

That's all she would say about my father, and when I was little, that was enough. I hardly ever thought about him.

Our family stories were recycled endlessly, and whenever my mother told me about how I'd been named, she usually added another story wrapped around the first. She'd expected me to be a girl, so she hadn't been prepared with any boys' names as possible alternatives to the dreadful Eugene Charles. She'd been forced to dream up Keith Lee right there on the spot in her hospital bed. If I'd been a girl *the way I was supposed to*, I would have been named Cynthia.

I never thought of myself as Cynthia, but I did play at being a girl sometimes, painted myself with my mother's lipstick and traipsed around the apartment in her clothes and high heels, although that didn't last very long because she got furious at me — not so much for dressing like a girl as for *making a mess*. Once she got so mad at me that she made me promise to stay out of her stuff, and to make sure that I did, she gave me an old rouge and lipstick to play with. Then, as I got older, my mother's clothes lost their appeal. When I was playing at being a girl, I didn't want to look like a grown-up lady; I wanted to look like the girls my own age.

MY MOTHER WENT OFF to work, but my grandmother stayed home. She was the one who dressed me before I could dress myself, took care of me when I got sick, fed me breakfast, lunch, and dinner, baked me treats like pies and cookies and tarts, and kept every inch of our apartment clean. Working took a lot out of my mother; she often came home with a sick headache, went to bed with a cold cloth over her eyes, but my grandmother never seemed to get sick. She talked to me constantly.

"You see," she would say, "Dad had his boat tied up in West Wheeling, and the railroad ran down to the river. I'd go with him at noon. In the train, he'd take me down with the engineer, and I'd stand there with the engineer, and we'd ride to West Wheeling and get on Dad's boat. We carried nails and tobacco. The boats were very small, built with a pilot house and a cabin. We were always up in the pilot house, had to stay where Dad could see us, you know. I pretended I was steering the boat . . ."

That was the story at the center of all her stories. My grandmother never got tired of telling it, just as I never got tired of hearing it. She was a little girl, standing on a box in front of her father, Everett Thomas, the river boat captain. He was piloting his boat down the Ohio River, but her hands were on the wheel too. In her make-believe world, she was the pilot.

She would stop what she was doing in the kitchen, step out onto the sun porch with me. Her hands would be red from the hot water; she would dry them on a tea towel. "The wheel was round, big as that doorway," pointing to show me, "maybe bigger."

She would sweep her arm in an arc across the sun porch windows. "The whole top was windows," creating the pilot house for me. "There was this gadget to tell the engine room how to go." She would draw it in the air. "A string from the ceiling for the whistle. You gave it a little tug for one toot, or two toots, or whatever. You had to blow your whistle right around Wheeling —"

She would stand there a moment, looking out at the river. "Well," she would say — that single word she used to sum up the entire universe.

HER NAME WAS Mabel Idona Thomas. If you asked her middle name, she would shrug and say, "I don na," a joke she must have been making all of her life. She was born in 1886, so in my childhood memories of her she would have been in her early sixties — a vigorous woman at the height of her power. She had the squared-off, truculent, bulldog jaw of the Thomases and pale eyes that snapped with blue light. She read the Bible every day but never discussed religion. Her personal motto, often repeated, was: "It's a great life if you don't weaken."

Growing up with her was like having an open window on the nineteenth century. The fire engine that clanged up the street, sirens wailing, was "the hook and ladder," and the massive hunk of Victorian furniture that stood in her bedroom was a "chifferobe" — a word I've found in no dictionary. She had dozens of sayings that defined the world for me. When anyone in the family started a sentence with "If," musing about what could have been, she would say, "Well. If my aunt had balls, she would have been my uncle."

She could always make me laugh even if it sometimes took me years to figure out her jokes. She would refer to a lovely piece of classical piano music called "Clar de Saloon" or burst into the popular song from Carmen:

> Torayadora,
> Don't spit on the floor!
> Use the cuspidor,
> That's what it's for.

"What's a cuspidor?" I asked her.

"It's another name for a spittoon," she told me. "It was a big brass pot the men spit their tobacco into back in the old days," and later, when she saw one standing in a corner of a shop, made sure to point it out to me: "*That's* a cuspidor."

"Where was Moses when the lights went out?" she would sometimes call out to me. Gleefully, I'd yell back the correct answer: "Down in the basement eating sauerkraut!"

BEFORE SHE GAVE UP her shop and came to take care of my mother and me, my grandmother had been a seamstress and was proud of it. The whole "out-the-pike crowd" — that meant the rich folks — used to come to her shop to get clothes made or alterations done, and she made clothes for me and my mother all the time. She could make any Halloween costume I could imagine; all I had to do was show her a picture. She taught me to sew with a needle and thread when I was so little that it felt like something I'd always known how to do, and I spent hours sitting on the floor of our sun porch cutting up scraps of cloth and sewing them together to make pretty patterns. I loved the feeling of the different fabrics under my fingertips — velvet was my favorite — and I loved playing with my grandmother's sewing machine. She told me a million times to *be careful*, and I *was careful*, but you'd have to be magnificently stupid in order to run the needle through your fingers. The machine wouldn't go if the needle was raised up, and if the needle was lowered, you'd have to force your fingers under a little metal gadget to get them anywhere near the needle, so I knew I was safe. I sewed things together on the machine lickety-split — Z I P.

From time to time she would take me to town. She dressed properly for these occasions, wore a hat and gloves as a lady should, and we always visited the ladies' wear departments in the big stores so she could see what was "on the market." She would take a dress or a skirt off the rack, flip it inside out, and show it to me. "Good Lord, Keith," she'd say, "can you believe the finish work on this?" She'd show me how the seams were crooked or threads had been left unclipped or the lining wasn't very nice or the zipper hadn't been sewn in well. "I can't believe what they're selling to the public these days," she'd say, shaking her head. "Can you believe anything this shoddy? And they expect people *to pay for it.*"

It was fun for a few minutes, but it always went on longer than I could stand it — as we studied things that grown-up ladies wore, looking for what was wrong with them. Of course I knew what cotton, linen, rayon, corduroy, hopsacking, silk, satin, velvet, velveteen, and tulle were — didn't everybody? Of course I knew that you only got what you paid for and that it was better to put your money into quality merchandise rather than buy some dumb thing that was going to fray and fall apart the first time you "warshed" it.

You could tell people by their clothes. "Who does she think she is?" my grandmother would say about a lady who was too dressed up. Even worse was a lady who "let herself go." That's what ladies did sometimes when their husbands died or ran around. *Ran around where?* I wondered. You could tell that a man was a gentleman by the pattern of his tie, the cut of his suit, the condition of his fingernails. Some slick fellow in cheap shiny shoes and a badly fitted suit looked, my grandmother said, like "a snake-oil salesman." Children got blamed on their mothers. "Can you imagine her mother dressing her like that? Well." Girls could be dressed too young — a little bitty skirt on a great big girl — or too old — stockings and lipstick on a kid who hadn't got her figure yet. Little boys could be categorized just as quickly, and one glance could tell my grandmother whether a boy was somebody I could play with or not. For me, the most important thing about clothes was that's how you could tell who was a boy and who was a girl.

I'VE ALWAYS HAD the impulse to tell stories. It must have started with wanting to hear stories. When I was little, my mother put me to bed by telling me the adventures of Bucky the Bug, a tale that she made up on the spot. "You never minded going to bed," my mother told me. "You always wanted to hear the next part of the story." Those summer nights, as they settled down on me, felt as huge as continents. The light would be fading out at the windows; I'd be tucked into bed but not sleepy yet, and my mother would be telling me what was happening to Bucky the Bug *right now*. When my mother stopped telling me stories, I begin to tell them to myself. The first object I ever held in my hand was a pencil — that's the family legend — and as soon as I could, I began to notate my stories with stick figures. I spent so much time drawing that I developed a thick callus on the middle finger of my right hand.

The lower halves of our bathroom walls were tiled. Each tile — cream-colored and blank — looked to me like the panel of a comic strip. I'd sit on the bathroom floor and draw on the tiles with a soft lead pencil, filling in each one with the drawing that went with the story I was telling myself, working my way around the bathroom walls until I had filled all of the tiles as high as I could reach. Every evening my grandmother would scrub them clean with Ajax Cleanser so I could start over the next day and do it again. I felt no sense of loss when my comic strips were wiped away. I loved waking up in the morning knowing that I had all those shining blank tiles to fill.

When I got older, I moved from bathroom tiles to paper. I drew endless pictures of girls. If anybody had given me the "draw-a-person" test that psychologists sometimes use as an indicator of a child's gender identity, I would have drawn a girl without a moment's hesitation. I also clipped pictures of girls from the magazines lying around our apartment — *The Ladies' Home Journal* or *The Saturday Evening Post*. In the brightly-colored cartoon advertising of the day little daughters often appeared with their moms to stare in delight and amazement at some gleaming new kitchen appliance, and those were the girls I wanted to look like.

It's hard for me to re-create what I thought about boys and girls. Putting it into any words at all will automatically clear up at least some of the confusion I remember, but the confusion is what feels true to me. I didn't see much difference between boys and girls except for the length of their hair and the clothes they wore. So if you cut off a girl's hair and put her in pants, she would be a boy, or if you let my hair grow out and put me in a dress, I would be a girl. But, all the same, I could sense that there was something more to it than that, although I couldn't imagine what it could be. The older I got, the more it bothered me.

I AM THE PRODUCT of two failed marriages. I was raised by two women who, for very good reasons, did not trust men. Neither did I. When we met men on the street, my grandmother would say, matter-of-factly, "He's afraid of men," as I hid behind her. Nothing about men felt right to me; they were too big and thick, their voices too deep, and I wouldn't talk to them or even look at them. I just wanted them to go away.

My uncle Bill didn't come to visit us often, but when he did, he was like a dog that can sense your fear, and he always came straight for me. My mother would say, "Oh, Bill, don't tease him," but he never paid the slightest bit of attention to her. He'd chase me all over the apartment as I ran from him, crying. He seemed to think it was a great game. I'd crawl under chairs, trying to get away from him; I'd hide behind the couch or run into my room and try to hold the door shut, but he always caught me and held me, struggling in his arms, crying. Until he let me go, I couldn't get away from him. Laughing, he'd say, "You don't like me, do you?" He stunk of something—a thick, nauseating, sweetish scent I thought was the distinctive smell of *men*. Years later I would realize that it was the smell of whiskey.

Aunts and uncles came in sets of two like salt and pepper shakers. When you spoke of them, you ran their names together into a single unit — Martha'nHarley, Addie'nDee — and the other half of my scary uncle Bill was my gentle aunt Eleanor. She was blonde and blue-eyed like nearly everyone else in my family except for me. Trying to see her now, I find in my memory a small snapshot so drenched in sunlight that she looks radiantly blonde, impossibly blonde. She's swinging on the glider with my cousin Billy cuddled up on her lap, his head resting on her shoulder. She's stroking his hair and talking to another grown-up, probably my mother. I don't know much about my aunt Eleanor. Her family was German a generation or two back. She acted in amateur theater, and years later I would find a play script with her notes in the margin. I liked and trusted her, thought of her as my favorite aunt.

Bill'nEleanor's kids, Becky and Billy, were my closest cousins. Billy was a year younger than I was, Becky four years older and loud like her dad. She liked to boss me and Billy around, and she could be mean sometimes, but she could also be lots of fun, could dream up great games for us to play — get us dressed up like pirates looking for treasure or build a play house out of cardboard boxes so we could crawl inside and pretend it was a submarine.

Billy and I were often left on our own together. We were natural allies and got along just fine. Unlike me, he'd been named after his father — he was *William Henry Sharp the Fourth*, as he told me frequently, proud of it. His mom and dad always called him by his nickname "Binky," but he didn't like it if I called him that, so I didn't. Because I was older, we spent a lot of our time doing what I wanted to do — coloring or snipping pictures from magazines. We must have made an odd pair. I was small and brown-eyed, and when I felt safe, talkative. He was big, plump, blonde, blue-eyed, and didn't have much to say — although he talked to me. He felt like an almost little brother — someone who'd always been around and always would be.

## 4

MY FIRST PLAYMATE, my first real friend who wasn't a cousin, was Arlene, the girl who lived in the apartment directly above us. She always seemed bigger and more mature than I was, and I thought it wasn't fair that I'd never catch up — no matter how hard I tried, she'd always be one year older. She had lustrous black hair — not *almost* black but a true black like a crow's wing — and big flashing chocolate-brown eyes to go with it. As mothers often did to their daughters, her mom wound Arlene's hair into tight, perfectly formed tubes to give her the fat glossy curls that were admired on little girls in those years just after the war. I sat in their kitchen, watched her do it, marveled at how much time it took — so long that Arlene would begin to fidget. Years later, when I would hear the song that said, "and her hair hung down in ringlets," I would think of Arlene. Because I was a brown-eyed kid in a blue-eyed family, it mattered to me that she had brown eyes like mine.

I remember Arlene in the full-skirted dresses of the time, plaids and ginghams. I admired how polished she looked when she was on her way to church — her hair freshly curled, dressed in patent leather shoes and a navy coat — and I thought that if I turned out to be a girl, that was exactly how I'd want to look. We played together in her apartment or in mine, or, if the weather was nice, outside in the yard. We were strictly forbidden to cross the street or go near the river.

Arlene had several girlfriends her own age who came over to play, so then it was me and the girls. We played what I would later see as "girls' games," but we called them "make-believe" or "pretend games" to differentiate them from physically active things like hide-and-seek or red rover. We pretended to be other people and acted out their stories. I'm so far back in time that all I can find are a few unfocused images, but I can remember the girls dressing me up in costumes assembled from Arlene's old clothes. In the make-believe families we were creating it was easy for me to play the youngest daughter — a role that felt natural to me.

I was with Arlene the first time I saw a naked human being other than myself. The Josephs were the other family living upstairs in our building, and they had a baby girl. Once, when Mrs. Joseph gave the baby a bath, Arlene and I watched. What sticks in my memory, what really surprised me — struck me as odd and not right at all — was that Mrs. Joseph put the wrong kind of soap in the bathtub. It came in a box — in flakes that had a sneaky viscous feeling to them. You dumped a bunch into your wash machine, and when you ran the water on them, they frothed up and made a foam — they were called "Ivory Snow" — and she threw some of these into the bathtub, and put the stopper in, and ran the bathtub full of water, and it filled with suds just as though she was going to wash her clothes, but she wasn't going to wash her clothes, she was going to wash her daughter, and I thought, this can't be right, can it? Won't it hurt the baby?

The baby loved being in the bathtub with the Ivory Snow; she splashed around in the warm water and made little cooing noises. I can remember quite clearly what she looked like. There was nothing between her legs at all, but I didn't think, oh, she's *a girl*, she's different from me. I thought, oh, she's *a baby* — this is what a baby looks like, so I must have looked exactly like that when I was a baby — but really, it wasn't the main thing on my mind. I was more worried about the Ivory Snow than I was about human bodies. The words from a girls' jump-rope chant pretty well summed it up for me:

> Fudge, fudge, call the judge.
> Mommy had a baby.
> Not a boy. Not a girl.
> Just a plain old baby!

I WAS SICK so much as a child that they bought me a bed table and a special wedge-shaped pillow so I could sit up in bed and draw. I had to take unbelievably nasty blue pills called "Pyribenzamine," and my grandmother would smear my chest with Vicks VapoRub, cover it with a layer of cotton, then a layer of cloth — thin T-shirt material. She'd set the vaporizer going in the corner of my bedroom; it hissed quietly, making everything steamy and scented of camphor. She turned on the radio for me — a box made of Bakelite with a green dial. Voices from the radio told me stories as I drew my own stories. Sometimes I had fever dreams as thick with images as wallpaper. In my earliest years I had visitations that were worse than nightmares.

Night terrors occur in the early part of the sleep cycle when there's no rapid eye movement. They afflict toddlers and young children and can be deeply frightening to the observing adults if they don't know what's happening — as my mother and grandmother didn't. Adults often describe the children as looking possessed. They cry out. They're deeply distressed and sometimes stare fixedly at something just beyond their field of vision. Most children, when they have night terrors, don't remember them, but I remembered mine. My mother and grandmother kept saying, "Look at his eyes, look at his eyes, look at his eyes." I don't know what my version of "Oh, my God!" would have been, but that's what I was feeling. My mother and grandmother's voices sounded rumbly, echoey, as though they were in another room, a huge one with stone walls. I couldn't move a muscle — *Wrong with my eyes, wrong with my eyes, what could be wrong with my eyes?* — heard them saying over and over again, "Look at his eyes." *My eyes, my eyes?*

Another time it was a shower of pins that were many different colors. They weren't nice colors, like rainbow colors; they were sharp nasty colors — blue and black and red — and they were falling in a thick cloud of little pins all lined up together, not dispersed, coming down all together. From the way I was seeing them, they were above me and to the left — a countless number, millions of tiny pins raining down on me, trying to do something horrible to me. I don't know how long I had night terrors, but they made the night dangerous. I tried to keep them out by pushing on the front door to hold it shut. I might have sleepwalked there; I was not fully awake — I know that — and the radiating glow of that awful yellow light, threatening, disgusting, smeared through the curtain. I drew that shower of pins. "Like that, like that. It looked like that."

### 6

AFTER MY MOTHER had exhausted her imagination on the tale of Bucky the Bug, she began reading to me. We went through horse books, dog books, and the Hardy Boys; about these stories I remember absolutely nothing.

Then she must have decided to try the classics, so she moved on to *Tom Sawyer*. I remember liking it, but, except for the scene in which Tom gets lost in a cave with the golden-haired Becky Thatcher, little of it has stuck in my head. But her next choice, *Huckleberry Finn*, was exactly right. Reading it again now, I've found, to my astonishment, that I recall it as vividly as if I'd heard it only last month — not a lifetime ago. *Huckleberry Finn* was my first big, important, serious book — my ur-text. For however many nights it took for my mother to read the story, I was saturated with Twain's world.

Writing fiction is not about words on paper; it's about creating a space where people can live — as I lived inside that story I heard when I was five. The river running through *Huckleberry Finn* was, simply, *our* river, and the story flowing through it was an eternal *now*. Huck Finn and Jim on their raft were floating on the river I could see through our sun porch window. I knew that people caught catfish in the river and ate them, and I knew that people drowned in the river. I learned from Huckleberry Finn that a drowned man dead in the water floats face down. I learned that you can bring bodies up by firing cannons across the top of the water. I learned that if you took loaves of bread and cut them open and put bits of quicksilver in the center of the bread, the bread would flow to where the corpse was in the water. This all made perfect sense to me, was bone-deep in me, because the river was right there, rolling by us. People did drown in the river, and I had always been warned to stay away from it — *"Don't go in the river."* But the river was the center of everything. This is the most fundamental fact of me, the farthest down I can get — I was a kid who grew up on an island in the middle of a river.

The sinister grown men in Huck Finn resonated with my own fear of grown men. When the Duke and the King first turn up in the story, I found them so scary that I asked my mother to stop. "Oh, come on, honey," she said, "give it a chance. Just keep on with a little bit more. It'll get better," and it did. I was glad that she kept on reading right on through to the end.

I was fascinated by the scene in which Huck dresses up like a girl. Because I was never sure that I was really a boy, the distinction between *playing* a girl and *being* a girl — however important it is from an adult point of view — was, in my child's mind, blurry at best, but Twain makes it clear what Huck is doing. I knew that he hadn't turned into a girl *for real*, that he was only pretending.

Huck and Jim are hiding out, so they have to be careful not to give themselves away, but they need to find out what the people in the town are saying about them. They've found some old clothes in a trunk, so Huck rolls up his trousers, puts on a calico dress and a bonnet, practices so he can walk around in the outfit, and goes to the nearest farmhouse to talk to the grown-up lady there. She figures out pretty quick that he's a boy because he makes several mistakes. When he threads a needle, he holds the thread steady and tries to poke the needle onto the thread. I knew better than that — that

35

you're supposed to hold the needle steady. I even knew that you're supposed to lick the thread first. Then the lady gives Huck a twisted piece of lead to throw at a rat, and he throws like a boy and almost hits it, but I could never make that mistake. I'd heard yelled at me a million times: "You throw like a ga-rul!" And then, when the lady tests him out by throwing the piece of lead onto his lap, he doesn't spread his skirt like a girl; he slams his knees together like a boy. That was a hard one. If it happened in a flash, how could you make yourself remember that you were wearing a skirt so you'd spread it out to catch something? Maybe you'd have to wear a skirt a lot to be able to do that, but I told myself I'd try my best to remember. I'd already pretended to be a girl lots of times — either alone or playing with Arlene and her friends — and there was no doubt in my mind that sometime in the future I would pretend to be a girl again. Or maybe I was a girl for real. But either way, I wanted to be able to *do it right*.

**7**

WE HAD A BIG framed picture on our living room wall. It had been there forever, and I had spent hours looking at it, but I could never figure out the story. I knew that there were lots of things I couldn't understand because I was too little, and that picture was one of them. It gave me the creeps. As blue as things got at twilight on the Ohio River, they never got as weirdly blue as that, so it had to be some story-book place, and I didn't like it. Nothing felt right — not the enormous leafy tree with its branches hanging down nor the thick lumps of dead stone nor the distant forbidding mountains with no roads or houses on them.

Lying on the front porch of a big house was a pretty girl wearing her bathrobe. She was lying on her back with an arm folded over her forehead, and a boy was standing next to her, looking straight down at her. I could tell from the expression on his face that he wanted something — for her to wake up, maybe, and talk to him. I knew he was a story-book boy because his hair was too long for a real boy's but not as long as a girl's. He was bent forward, his hands on his knees. He was as naked as a jaybird.

"What is that boy *doing?*" I asked my mother.

"Oh, honey," she said, laughing at me, "they're both girls," and I looked at the picture for a long time.

*That picture had always been there on our living room wall.* It was a part of reality as it had been given to me, as eternal as the couch or the kitchen table — as eternal as my mother and grandmother themselves. They must have *wanted* it there on the wall, so it had to mean something. I asked her to tell me the story.

"It's dawn," she said. It wasn't the front of somebody's house but the front of a temple. The older girl wasn't wearing a bathrobe; she was wearing the kind of clothes they wore in ancient times. She was having a dream, and the naked little girl was only part of the dream.

37

What a dumb story. Why would anybody make a picture about that? I wasn't going to argue with her, but I knew that my mother was wrong about the boy. He was *not* a girl. I knew he was a boy because he felt like me, or I felt like him — or something. What I would say now is that I identified with him. He was the only thing in the picture I liked.

Then my mother tried it another way. The naked person was *the dawn itself*.

Trying to get a preschooler to understand a personification is a fairly tall order, and she never succeeded with me. The best I could do was to imagine a court — a king and queen and their people who were in charge of everything — and somebody says, "Okay, it's time for the dawn," so they send someone to start the dawn, and the person they send is the boy in the picture. Then he could be saying to the girl, "Wake up, honey, I'm starting the dawn." But there was no way I could see him as *the dawn itself*.

Twenty-some years later, in a bookstore in Harvard Square, I'd flip through the pages of a big, glossy coffee-table book and see that wacky picture again, feel the queasy lurch in my stomach that hits me whenever I stumble upon some lost fragment of my childhood. Then I would discover that we weren't the only family in the world to have Maxfield Parrish's "Daybreak" on our wall. It was one of the most popular art prints ever produced in America. As I stared at the picture, I felt again something of the confusion and anxiety I'd felt as a kid.

The figure that my child's eyes had seen as a boy like me was obviously a slender girl of about ten or eleven — smooth-skinned, androgynous, and faintly blue — wearing a short twenties bob and nothing else.

## 8

MY GRANDMOTHER ENCOURAGED in me a certain delicacy, even a prissiness, but she wasn't going against my grain — at least a part of me was that way naturally. She liked it when I was doing what I liked to do best — sitting quietly, sewing or drawing or cutting out pictures. She was obviously pleased when grown-ups said, astonished, "He never gets dirty!" I think now that she was of that generation and mindset of women who liked to imagine little boys as pure, pretty, angelic, and as *sexless* as they thought girls were, who dressed their sons in Lord Fauntleroy suits or even exactly like their sisters, as did Hemingway's mom, thus sending Ernest down the rocky road toward becoming — at least on the surface — one of the most absurdly macho writers in American literature.

We were living in the 1940s, not the 1890s, so there were limits to how my grandmother could present me to the world — and I was also picking up social cues from other kids so there were limits to how I would allow myself to be presented — but my grandmother shoved me into the bath every day, sometimes a flower-scented bubble bath, and taught me how to use a nail brush, a toothbrush, and a hair brush. She ironed everything I owned, including my T-shirts and handkerchiefs. Because I was sickly, she made me wear snowsuits for a year longer than any other boy my age, which made me cringe with embarrassment. She kept my hair long for a boy, gave me a manicure once a week, and painted my nails with clear polish, and that was just fine with me — I liked my nails shiny. Once, when I was very little, she bought me plain brown shoes with straps that buckled, much like the ones worn by Christopher Robin in *Winnie the Pooh*. I knew that girls wore shoes like that but boys didn't — at least no boys that I ever saw — and I liked them but already knew enough to know that I *shouldn't* like them, so I didn't wear them often.

As far back as I could remember, grown-ups had been saying about me, "He's like a girl," and I took it as a compliment. I *liked* being like a girl — was proud of it — and would have been even more like a girl if I'd had the chance, but as soon as I left our apartment, I could feel the world pushing back at me. My uncle Bill even called me a sissy once. It was the first time I remember that word ever being used to shame me. What he actually said was, "You're *a big sissy*." I couldn't have been any more hurt if he'd hit me.

But there was more to me than just a little boy sitting on the floor sewing brocade roses onto black velvet. I was also an active and fearless kid. I remember flinging myself bodily down stairs, taking whole thoughtless runs of them in a single bound, flinging myself over the porch railing, all of me up and over — C H A Z A M! Hurt myself? Are you kidding?

The game was played like this: first you climb up the side of the back porch — no, I don't mean *climb*, I mean you throw your whole blessed body up there, paw and scrabble, claw your way up there — then you run across the porch as fast as you can, and you jump over the edge. NO, DON'T STOP TO THINK. You run around the yard and do it again. Sometimes BING, it's reversed — okay, now you do it all backwards. There's the lattice where the flowers will grow; fling yourself down it, grab a tickle of a hand hold, of a foot hold, of a just-enough hold as it flicks by, because that's all it takes — no way you can career out of control; no way you can go splat on the ground — because you go up, you go down, you go over, you go everywhere just as quick as a wink. Arlene and I played that game with other kids, both boys and girls. I remember laughing and yelling the whole time. We were never hurt. I felt fast and smart inside my body.

ALL I KNEW about Wheeling, West Virginia, was that it was my home; I took everything about it as just the way things were. Wheeling was an industrial town with steel mills, chemical plants, and glass works lining both sides of the river. I loved riding up the river road at night, seeing the eerie flames of the open-hearth furnaces blazing away, looking exactly the way I imagined hell.

Sometimes rains fell on us that were more acidic than battery acid and the air pollution created fogs so thick that if I walked with my mother out to the middle of the Suspension Bridge, we wouldn't be able to see either shore. Sleet, hail, freezing rain, and wet snow fell on us in the winter; high humidity and fierce heat stifled us in the summer. Mosquitos swarmed up from the river at twilight and bit the living daylights out of us. Once we had a plague of toads, so many that cars squished them into a slippery mulch and skidded.

But I also remember days as perfect as circles. From our sun porch window I could look across the front river to the downtown where a few streets, parallel to the river, rose until the hills became too steep for them. In the summer those background hills were an eye-blistering green, in the autumn an enchanted quilt-work of yellows and reds. We were at the bottom of the valley, on a floodplain, and every year or two the river rose up and flowed over us. In the first flood I remember, the water rose so high that our basement flooded and the tops of the clothesline poles out in the backyard barely cleared the water. A neighbor rowed up to our back door and asked if we would like anything from the store. My grandmother made a list, gave it to me, walked me partway down the back stairs, and lowered me into the rowboat. I was proud that I was the one to bring home the groceries. Then, as it always did, the river went back down. The neighbors came out with their garden hoses, squirted away the thick piles of mud. You'd be surprised how cheery everybody was. Floods? Of course we knew all about floods. We lived on *the Island*.

Floodplains have always been attractive because they're so fertile, and the elite of the first white settlers farmed on the Island and built themselves fine homes there. Later on, when "out the pike" became the place for the rich folks to live, they moved and left their houses behind — many with classic Appalachian front porches flanked by columns — and there they are in my memory, a bit rundown and shabby, but nice, neighborly. Some of those old houses had been subdivided into apartments like the first one where I lived with my mother and grandmother — so old that it still had the fixtures for gas lamps on the walls.

The south end of the Island was working class; the north end, where we were, was lower middle class, seedy genteel. Our neighborhood ran from the end of the Suspension Bridge north up to the narrow tip called "Belle Isle," extended west from the river as far as Virginia Street. The same people had been there forever, and everybody knew everybody. Children could roam freely, and nobody thought a thing about it. It was inconceivable that anyone would deliberately hurt a child. In the summer I'd get up, get dressed, have breakfast, and then walk out of our apartment and wander.

I didn't become a solitary loner until I was well into grade school. I was quite sociable and knew all the kids my own age. Hopscotch was a girls' game, but if I wanted to play, that was okay with them. Skip rope games were a different matter — they were absolutely *for girls only*. I loved watching them, though — especially when they'd get a piece of rope as long as a clothesline and a whole line of girls would jump, rising and falling like a wave.

I naturally related to people by *talking* to them, and I felt more at home with girls than I did with boys, but there was a passel of boys who lived around Front Street, and they included me in their group. Some of them even liked me well enough to stop by our house looking for me. One of their dads built us a platform halfway up a tree. We called it our "tree fort," and of course no girls were allowed there. In the summer I dressed just like the other boys — in khaki shorts, horizontally striped T-shirts, and the high-top black sneakers we called "basketball shoes." Unlike the other members of my family who had to be careful in the sun, I never burned but simply turned brown. Unless they looked at me closely enough to notice the clear nail polish I might still have been wearing, anybody would have seen me as a perfectly ordinary Wheeling Island boy.

But right from the beginning I knew that I wasn't like other boys — "not a real boy" I said in my mind and told no one about it. When I was with the other boys, I tried to act like them, but it was hard work. Boys were supposed to be able to catch balls; I'd tried, but I couldn't do it. I wouldn't know about it until I'd have my eyes tested at eight, but I was extremely nearsighted — anything farther away from me than a few feet was a blur — so when anybody threw a ball at me, I couldn't see it coming until it was practically smacking me on the nose, and I certainly couldn't catch it. The best I could do — and half the time I couldn't even manage that — was jump out of the way at the last possible moment so it wouldn't hit me, so I never played softball or football, but I loved the pick-up games that boys and girls could play together, like "kick the can" or "red rover" or good old "hide and go seek." Sometimes I could lose myself entirely in games like that.

The moms would call their kids back at lunchtime or dinner time or, worst of all, at bedtime. You'd hear them calling in loud voices — "Arlene!" "Karen Sue!" "Bobby!" "Keith!" Some of the moms stood out on their back porches and rang bells or banged on pieces of metal, and we might be halfway up Front Street or down by the dangerous river where we weren't allowed to go; the twilight might be settling in, the sky going smoky gray-blue, and we'd know that we'd have to run home soon and go to bed. Our time was ending because our moms were calling us — a whole chorus of moms — but we were still playing playing playing because that's all that mattered. It was more than just a game — anybody who's ever been there knows that. Maybe we could make it last a little bit longer. Aw, Mom, I'll be home in a minute. Aw, come on, Mom, have a heart on a guy.

The City of Wheeling had a whacking big air-raid siren. When they'd blown that siren during the war, everybody had turned out all their lights so the Nazis and Japs couldn't see to bomb the city. We'd won the war, so there were no planes left up there to bomb us, but they still blew that siren every night at ten o'clock. Under a city bylaw, children were not allowed out on the street after ten — that was called "the curfew" — and when they blew that darned siren, we had to go home. If you got old enough, you didn't have to obey the curfew. We didn't know how old that was, but it was a lot older than we were, so no matter where you were or what you were doing, no matter how much fun you were having, when you heard that wail, you had to drop everything and run. After the curfew, the cops drove around the streets slowly, looking for loose children, and I ran home more than once, eating my own heartbeat. When you heard the siren, that wasn't just your mom making you go home — that was *the City of Wheeling* making you go home.

**9**

I WOULD NOT KNOW until many years later that my father had been a tap dancer, but tap links my story to his in a way that feels stronger than mere coincidence. I must have just turned six when I saw tap for the first time. I was with my aunt Eleanor and my cousin Billy at the annual recital of one of our local dance schools. I don't remember seeing my cousin Becky on the stage, but she must have been in the recital — otherwise there would have been no reason for us to be there.

It was in the Capitol Theatre near the end of the Suspension Bridge — one of Wheeling's historic landmark buildings — and I remember being fascinated by the two statues of ladies that were set into alcoves above and on either side of the stage. The ladies were wearing only a thin winding of fabric, and their entire bodies were stretched upward, their arms extended above their heads. They were apparently using every fiber of their beings to press bowls upward toward the sky, and I thought, *why on earth are they doing that?* For years I was puzzled by those ladies.

Eventually, the recital started. Billy and I couldn't read yet, so Aunt Eleanor whispered to us, explained where we were in the program. I thought of all the people I saw on the stage as "big kids" — much older than I was. I loved the ballet girls in their straight-out puff skirts and shiny pink shoes with pink ribbons. I was amazed that they could dance on the very tips of their toes; I saw it as both beautiful and scary. And I was blown away by the numbers done in black light — those fantastic, delicious moments when the stage went dark and I saw brilliantly colored lines moving around rather than kids. I loved the black light so much that I was disappointed whenever they didn't use it.

Near the end, there was a tap number I remember with hallucinatory clarity. I've told the story to myself so often that I've underlined it in my mind; when I go back to it now, I can't tell what's the original event and what's *the underlining*, but whatever I've got, here it is.

There was nothing unusual in the way it started. It was just a line of big girls. Now I'd guess that they were my cousin Becky's age — about ten. They tapped onstage in a single line and never broke apart, continued to address the audience in that single line. I remember getting the point of tap — the rhythmic element of it — loving the click of their taps on the wood. The girls wore lots of bright makeup, short Shirley Temple dresses, white socks, and the classic black patent tap shoes tied with bows. They had perfect and absolutely identical shiny blonde sausage curls, and they did every cute step and gesture you would expect from girls on stage in 1948. While they tapped, they sang, and I don't remember any of the words, but the tune was bubbly and cheerful and fast and fun. They went through their routine, ended it with an elaborate curtsy, and then reached up, grabbed their blonde sausage curls, snatched off their wigs, and revealed themselves as boys. The audience laughed and yelled and stomped and applauded. The boys bowed, waved their wigs, and ran offstage. I was shocked down to my toenails.

I already knew enough to know that I couldn't talk about this weird event to anybody, but I thought about it obsessively. What on earth kind of boys were they, anyway? Did they like getting dressed up like girls and dancing like girls for everyone to see, or had somebody made them do it? If somebody had made them do it, what could they have been threatened with horrible enough to make them do it? But if they'd liked doing it, why had they liked it? The grown-ups seemed to think it was funny, but I didn't think it was funny, why was it funny? How could you tell if all the girls in the other dance numbers were really girls? How could you tell that any girl was really a girl — or that any boy was really a boy?

10

AFTER MY MOTHER decided not to name me Eugene Charles after my father — *because I deserved my own name* — she named me after a character in a book. I'd always known that I was named for Keith Alexander — whoever he was. My mother said that when I got old enough, I could read all about him.

Then, after she'd got a K for my first name, she decided to move straight through the alphabet — K L M — and picked "Lee." Countless Southern children have been named "Lee" since the Civil War, but we weren't Southerners, and I don't think my mother had that connection in mind at all — it probably just sounded nice to her — but from my point of view, it was yet *another* lousy choice in names because it could belong to either a boy or a girl. When you tacked it onto my first name and said it quickly, it really did sound like a girl's name, and I hated being called Keith Lee and stopped anyone who tried to do it.

I was not happy with Keith either. In Wheeling in the late '40s, *nobody* was named Keith, and I wished

I had an ordinary name like the boys I knew — Billy, Eddie, Bobby, or Jack. And then there was the name I'd had before I was born — Cynthia — and I thought that was just as bad a name for a girl as Keith was for a boy. If I was a girl, I certainly wouldn't want to be called Cynthia; I'd want a name like Arlene, Nancy, Linda, or Susie. The K part of my name felt right to me — it was the first alphabet letter I'd learned — so, if I was a girl, I was probably Kathy. But *was* I Kathy?

Sex was naughty and dirty, something we should never *ever* talk about; everybody knew that — I'm down at the kid level now — and so it was the most fascinating topic in the world. My mother and grandmother were not the only grown-ups who never allowed themselves to be seen naked; it must have been a common practice. I can remember sitting on the river bank with several other boys, speculating endlessly on *what on earth* girls had between their legs. We didn't have a clue.

My own thoughts on the subject I kept to myself. I knew that babies had nothing between their legs because I'd seen one with my own eyes, so if boys and girls had something down there that made them different from each other, they must grow it later. That made sense because we all knew that people grew things when they got older, that boys would grow hair on their faces and girls would grow breasts. My mother and grandmother told me that I too would grow hair on my face when I became a man, but I wasn't at all sure that I wanted to become a man — or that I would automatically become one. People kept telling me that I was a boy — and that I'd damned well better act like one — but I knew that something was wrong somewhere, and I didn't trust anything anybody told me. This was not the same thing as wanting to be a girl. In order to want to be a girl, you have to be certain that you're not one already.

I've chased my memories in circles, and the most honest thing I can say about this pre-school boy-girl stuff is that I was lost in a blurry confusion. In those days playing ball was a central defining feature of boyhood, and I did not play ball. If I'd had normal vision, would I have felt differently about ball games? Probably, but I don't know. What I do know is that I detested ball games, especially boys-only ball games, and I participated in them only if I was forced to. Girls, however, were not expected to play ball, so if I was a girl, I was perfectly normal. I'd always been told that I was *delicate*. I'd been born too soon, had spent the first few weeks of my life in an incubator — whatever that was — and I got sick a lot and had to stay in bed, so that meant I was delicate, but lots of girls were delicate. Girls cried a lot, so if I was a girl, nobody would call me a cry-baby. If I was a girl, of course I would have liked playing with other girls when I was little, and I would have liked dressing up in girls' clothes and putting on lipstick. And if I was a girl, it wouldn't matter that I didn't have a father. In my mind, boys needed fathers but girls didn't.

So, no matter what anybody said, I might really be a girl. Why didn't I believe my mother and grandmother?

Well, I'd learned by then that grown-ups don't always tell kids the truth, and then there was another possibility that was more complicated. I knew the distinction between "accidental" and "on purpose," and if they were not telling me the truth, it might be, somehow, "accidental" — that is, they might not know any better. That was a standard phrase of my grandmother's: "Oh, he just doesn't know any better." They, and all the other grown-ups, might simply have got it wrong — just like my mother got it wrong about that picture on our living room wall, that boy she kept saying was a girl.

Maybe we would go to Dr. Strobel one of these days, and he'd check me out and say, "I'm sorry to have to tell you this, but he's a girl," and my mother and grand-mother would say, "Oh, is that right? Well, that makes sense. We always thought there was something funny about him." Then I'd be Kathy, and they'd let my hair grow out, and we'd go over to town and buy me dolls and dresses. And then what?

If I had found out that I was a girl, it would not have been the answer to my fondest hopes and dreams. I would not have responded with a child's equivalent of, "Oh, thank God!" As troubled and confused as I was, I'd become used to myself as a boy, and if I'd been allowed to choose, I might very well have decided to stay that way. But if it turned out that I was a girl, that would have been just fine with me and in many ways would have made my life easier. There were things I liked about being a boy, but sometimes the thought of being a girl felt just right.

What I wanted was to know for certain one way or the other. Of course it never occurred to me, or to anyone else at the time, that there might be more than two choices. The gender binary was so fundamental to our culture that it was impossible to conceive of anything else.

## 11

BEFORE I LEAVE the earliest years of my childhood, there's another story I have to tell — although I would rather not. "Fragment" is a word that's often applied to early memories, and this one really is a fragment — it has no context, is attached to nothing, simply sticks in my mind like a shard of broken glass. It's set in the basement of the apartment building at 14 North Front Street, and it has a "not in school yet" feeling to it. The best I can guess, it was the summer after I'd turned six.

Arlene and I were in the storage locker in the basement. I have a color snapshot stored in my autobiographical memory — a view from kid height, looking up. Arlene is taller than I am. She's standing on tiptoe, reaching to get something from a shelf. Then two boys are suddenly there with us. Arlene doesn't pay any attention to them, but I turn around to see what they want. They are much older than we are, so much older that I can't put numbers to it. My first thought is, *they don't belong here.*

I knew them of course. They lived a long way up the Island from us, came from the kind of families my grandmother called "no good." I remember them as lean, tall and wiry, burnt buckeye-brown from the sun, the kind of boys who wore basketball shoes so old the soles were loose and flapping. I have an image of an arm — the veins and muscles of it, the smear of brownish-black dirt all the way to the elbow. These were boys with a reputation. I was scared of them, but I thought they'd go away. They had no business in our basement, and if a grown-up caught them there, they'd be in big trouble. I couldn't imagine why they'd even come into our apartment building in the first place. It wasn't *their* building.

I can't remember how it started, but this is what they said: "Keith, you've got to learn how to treat a girl."

Arlene didn't seem scared at all. Girls, when they had to, could turn into miniature versions of their mothers, assume an air of insufferable superiority, and then their message to stupid, immature, unruly boys was, "Oh, you're just being silly." That's what Arlene was doing. I wasn't saying a word. "You know what a man does?" they said to me. "A man hits a girl."

I had to get out of there, but when I tried to run past them, one of them grabbed me and dumped me bodily back into the storage locker. Then he grabbed my arm, jerked it around behind my back, and levered it up, hurting me. This was a standard boy trick, a test. If you cried, you lost. I didn't cry. Then he grabbed the back of my neck and pinched — another standard boy trick. I was writhing with pain, but I still didn't cry.

Whatever she'd been getting from the shelf, Arlene had it. Then she tried to walk around the boys and leave. It never seemed to have occurred to her that she couldn't simply do that. They caught her and pushed her back into the storage locker. That changed everything. Her air of the miniature lady dropped away, and she went as silent as a stone. "You should hit her," they told me. "That's how men treat girls. Hit her."

I tried to talk my way out of it, but whatever I said, they just kept repeating, "No, no, no. A man hits a girl. Go on. Be a man. Hit her."

They kept showing me how to make a fist. One of them grabbed Arlene under the chin, tilted her face up, and offered it for me to hit.

All these years later I know what to call this incident. It was an assault. We all know about the fight or flight response; trauma specialists have added a third possibility — if you can't fight, and you can't flee, then you can freeze. That's what Arlene and I did. People who freeze often don't remember what happened, and I don't remember much more of it. The boys kept saying, "Be a man. Hit her," but I don't remember how long it lasted or if they did any more physical things to me. I'm guessing that I must have simply stood there, silent and frozen. Then, eventually, I must have given up. As gently as I could, I punched Arlene on the tip of her chin. She burst into tears and ran out. They let her go. They must have let me go too. I remember them laughing.

Assault survivors can often have a damnably difficult time processing what happened to them, and one of the strategies they can use — particularly if the event was utterly unexpected and utterly bizarre — is to tell themselves IT NEVER HAPPENED. That's what Arlene and I seemed to have done. Because it never happened, we never had to talk about it; we went on being friends just the way we had before. Because it never happened, I never told my mother or grandmother or anybody about it. Just as survivors often do, I suspected that it was my own fault. All the kids on the Island knew that I played with girls, that I liked girls, that I was *like a girl*, and that must have been the reason that those no-good boys had decided to pick on me. Maybe what they told me was the truth. If it was the truth, then I would never be a real boy.

## 12

I'D LONG AGO stopped asking, "Am I a boy or a girl?" because that had got me nowhere, had only made my mother and grandmother mad, but eventually I thought of a way to put the question that might be safe, that wouldn't automatically make my mother blow her top. "How can you tell a boy from a girl?"

The emotional charge of my need seems to have preserved not merely the information — that is, what I asked and what my mother answered — but the associated sensations: old brown varnished wood with a patch of sunlight on it — a wardrobe — and the smell of the wood from inside the open wardrobe door, a scent I now know as cedar. I remember late afternoon sunlight — slanting, golden. I'd just caught my mother in the midst of folding clothes, putting them away. I was trying my best to look like I could care less, as if what I'd just asked her was no more than a passing thought — "Oh, and by the way . . ." — but I could feel my desperation like a trip hammer. *How can you tell a boy from a girl?*

The first thing I could sense was her annoyance — now I'd use words like "resistance," "weariness" — but it felt exactly like what happened whenever I asked her about my father.

That was one of the most crucial moments of my childhood. I badly needed to know the answer. Because it was 1948 and I was six years old and had all the equipment that a boy was supposed to have, I did not need the complicated answer a progressive parent might give a child today. What I needed was some basic information about human anatomy. I needed to hear something like this: "You take their pants off and look at the stuff between their legs. *That's* how you tell the difference."

If she'd said that, then, of course, I would have asked her about the stuff between their legs, and my mother was no more capable of discussing that subject with me than she was of swimming the front river with a barbell strapped to her head. When she answered, she did it in a way that told me that the conversation was over — not just for that afternoon but forever. "Oh, honey," she said, "their bodies are different."

I stood there in that patch of golden late-afternoon sunlight and looked at my left hand. I wiggled my fingers. I could not tell by looking at my hand if it was a boy's hand or a girl's hand, and I was sure that nobody else could either. I was puzzled for a moment, and then I had an ah-ha experience. If you couldn't tell the difference between a boy and a girl just by looking at them, but if *their bodies were different*, then that difference must be something you couldn't see, something deep inside.

# part II

# ESMERALDA

**1**

AS A CHILD, I used crying as my major tactic for self-defense. Sometimes it worked, and sometimes it didn't. I was a Kindergarten wash-out, survived only two days, both of them spent weeping like a fountain. My grandmother announced to the principal, "He's not ready for school yet," and got her way as she usually did. I might have cried my way out of Kindergarten, but there was no way I could cry my way out of the first grade. "It's the law," my grandmother said.

I arrived in school already knowing the alphabet and how to spell a few words, and I was hungry to read. Our teacher divided us into two groups — the Blue Birds and the Red Birds. We weren't supposed to notice, but it was impossible not to, that the Blue Birds were learning to read faster than the Red Birds. After we'd been at it for a while, a third group was formed, the Black Birds — those kids who couldn't read a lick. I was the bluest of the blue; within weeks I went from not knowing how to read to being able to read almost anything. Forget Dick and Jane, I was puzzling my way through my mother's *Reader's Digests*. To say that I loved reading doesn't even get close to it; I read like a fire rips through a bone-dry forest. School was a waste of time because they wouldn't let me sit there all day reading. The moment I got home, I grabbed something and read it — and kept on reading until I fell asleep at night.

The day after our first report cards, our teacher rearranged our seats. We stood at the back of the room until our names were called. The kid with the highest grade in the class was seated in the first seat in the first row — and that was me. I sat down, put my stuff away in my desk, and turned around to see where the rest of the kids would go. A girl had the second highest grade in our class and was seated directly behind me. Her name was Nancy, and I remember her for her blonde sausage curls and startling ability to talk faster than anyone I'd ever met in my life. The seat behind Nancy went to a girl named Susanne. Both dismayed and not surprised at all, I watched the entire first row fill up with girls, and then I watched the second row begin to fill up with girls.

Halfway down the second row the first boy appeared — and then a few more. Eventually the teacher ran out of girls, and the seats in the last rows were filled with boys. The last seat in the last row was where the dumbest kid in the class had to sit. His name was Ricky. He'd been one of the Black Birds. He was taller, bigger, stronger, and meaner than any other boy in the first grade. He was so tall, big, strong, and mean that he could beat the crap out of boys years older than he was, and if he couldn't do it, his older brothers and sisters could. You didn't mess with Ricky.

After every report card, our teacher rearranged us so that all of us would know, all of the time, exactly how we were doing. I liked sitting near Nancy. I had a fierce crush on her, thought that she was just about as cute as a girl could be. She edged ahead of me a few times — she'd get the 98, and I'd get the 97 — and we'd trade seats; then, after the next report card, we'd trade them back. I spent the entire first grade in either the first seat or the second seat in the first row. At six, we were already being encouraged to compete with each other, but I never wanted to compete with anyone. I was never proud of my grades, didn't do anything to earn them — just did what I did, and my grades appeared. I felt a sense of what I would now call "inevitability." *Of course* I got high grades like a girl, so *of course* I was seated with the girls.

EVEN THOUGH I still didn't know with absolute certainty that I was a boy — even though I was like a girl in a million ways — I was stuck having to pretend to be a boy, and there was no way I could get out of it. I wasn't aware of any superior status attached to boys because there *was* no superior status attached to boys — not in those neat, orderly, oppressive classrooms run by nice middle-class white girls who'd grown up to be teachers. Just as I was meant to be, I was aware — acutely, keenly, cruelly — of the *differences* between boys and girls. That era we call "the '50s" was more complex and nuanced than it is often portrayed, but the gender split was just as bad as anyone remembers, and down at the kid level it was bad indeed. Everything under the sun was labeled "for boys" or "for girls" and then dealt out into two neat, mutually exclusive blue and pink piles. Adults didn't escape either. The gender binary had not been so emphatically emphasized since the nineteenth century.

During the war, women had been needed to work in the defense industries, and that muscular young woman we now remember as Rosie the Riveter — the one in the poster saying "We Can Do It!" — had been designed to recruit them. But we should also remember the other propaganda posters, the ones that personified what our boys were supposed to be fighting for — those idealized images of sweet young mothers and their adorable little daughters. Of course they were always white and as cutely feminine as you could imagine, mom and daughter often dressed alike. When the war ended, Rosie the Riveter's day was over; our boys needed jobs, and women were supposed to get out of the work force and go back to where they belonged — the home. Soon those images of perfect moms and daughters were everywhere, emblematic of the times.

In 1947 Christian Dior had introduced his "New Look," signaling an emphatic return to femininity. His full skirts, soft shoulders, and tiny waists forecast the styles that would evolve in the '50s. Nylon was no longer needed for the war effort, and American women shed their ankle socks for whisper-sheer nylon stockings. Technical advances made needle-thin high heels possible; constructed first of steel, then later of the newly developed plastics, they were called "spikes" or "stilettos" and soon became mandatory for formal occasions. Petticoats came back, then crinolines, along with severely cinched waists. These hyper-feminine styles matched the messages that were bombarding women from every direction — their role in life was domestic, their place was in the home, and they would find blissful fulfillment in becoming wives and mothers while their men went off each day and worked hard to support the whole damn works. Many American families weren't like that — mine certainly wasn't — and many people must have felt inadequate or abnormal for not fitting the stereotypes.

I remember plenty of girls who were what we would now call "girly girls," the ones who *did* fit the stereotypes, but I also remember a scary passel of tomboys on the Island — girls who ran like whippets, shinnied up trees, raced their bikes, got into violent mud fights on the river bank, and, in short, acted "like boys." They were not unusual. *The American Girl*, as an ideal type, had been socially constructed since at least the turn of the century, and she was supposed to be independent, adventurous, and active — to a degree. Everyone knew that she was going to grow up and get tamed someday. Everyone knew that by the end of the third act she would turn up transformed — scrubbed, powdered, perfumed, and decked out in a Cinderella ball gown — to win the heart of the hero and continue her life ever after as a good wife and mom. But those are all grown-up thoughts.

We were playing by kids' rules, and under those rules there was some room for a girl to be a tomboy but no room at all for a boy to be a sissy. If you were labeled as a sissy — if you were publicly acknowledged by all and sundry to be a sissy — that label hung around your neck forever like the rotting carcass of the kill made by a chicken-eating dog and your life was not worth living. I'd always known how to read people's social status by their clothes; now I became hyper-observant of other kids — and acutely aware of myself. How could I have allowed Arlene and her girlfriends to dress me up in Arlene's old clothes? That I'd only been four didn't seem to me an acceptable excuse; I told myself that I should have known better. Even worse, how could I have walked around in my mother's high heels or put on her lipstick? If anybody ever found out any of that stuff about me, I'd die of shame.

If you weren't paying close attention, even the tiniest little thing could give you away, and details that should have been less than trivial swelled up to the size of Mount Rushmore. When choosing snow boots for winter, I had to choose black ones, because girls sometimes wore brown. Colors were crucially important. Boys wore black, brown, and dark mossy shades. Plaids were okay, but you had to be careful because some of them — like Royal Stewart — were for girls. White was suspect; white shirts were okay, but white pants or shoes were definitely over the line. Blue was okay if it was dark enough, but all pastel colors were for girls. A boy could never, under any circumstances, wear red or pink. Of course I never talked about these things with anyone. Boys were not supposed to be interested in clothes.

Because I was sick so much of the time — and needed to stay warm, so said my grandmother — I had to wear knee socks. Even though no one could see them under my pants, I hated wearing them because knee socks were for girls. When I'd been little, I'd liked it when my grandmother painted my nails, but now I wouldn't let her do that because only girls wore nail polish. My nasal passages were firmly blocked throughout much of the winter, so I breathed through my mouth and got terribly chaffed lips. For several years one deep crack on the left side of my lower lip never quite healed — you can see it in all my school photographs — but I wouldn't allow anything to be put on it because only girls put things on their lips.

As many girls did, Arlene had a large collection of dolls; for every occasion, birthdays or Christmas, she'd get another one, and she'd always bring it downstairs to show us. I knew that she was proud of her dolls, and loved them, so I always told her that they were very nice. I'd learned by then that boys were supposed to say things like that to girls, just as they were supposed to say, "You look real pretty in that dress," but her dolls filled me with alarm. When I'd been little, I must have played with Arlene's dolls, but now I knew that I shouldn't hold them or even appear interested. Eventually her dolls began to radiate for me a powerful energy of intense, and repulsive, girlishness. Let alone hold them, I wouldn't even touch them — not even with a fingertip — for fear of being contaminated.

## 2

IT WASN'T FAIR. I'd been doing my best to act like a boy, but it hadn't worked. I'd been seated with the girls. When I read out loud, the teacher was always telling me to "speak up," and I tried, but I was scared the whole time I was in school, and I hated to have to stand up in the dreadful silence of the classroom with everybody looking at me, so my voice came out just above a whisper, and I could never get much volume out of it. I was sure that I sounded like a girl.

The books the teacher gave us were so easy it was pathetic; I never made a single mistake. Whenever Ricky was called on to read, he stood up all right, but he never said a word. He couldn't read at all. The teacher told me to take Ricky into the cloakroom and teach him to read.

The two kids who had been publicly labeled as the smartest and the dumbest in the first grade confronted each other in the cloakroom. That's where they sent you to punish you. It stunk in there, smelled like moldy sandwiches and wet filthy clothes and rubber boots. We didn't have any place to sit, stood facing each other, jammed up against the coats. I'd never before been so cruelly aware of how different I was from what I saw as *a real boy.*

I'm guessing now that it might have been Ricky's second try at the first grade. The main thing I remember about him is his sheer *massiveness.* He wasn't merely the biggest kid in our class; he was head and shoulders taller than the next biggest boy. Surely his voice couldn't have broken yet, but I remember it as almost a man's voice — deep and thick, dark and gravelly. His hands looked huge, big enough to squash my head. I can't swear that I was the smallest boy in our class, but I can't remember anyone smaller. Most of *the girls* were bigger than I was.

Both Ricky and I wanted to get out of that damned cloakroom. I tried my best to teach him to read, and he tried his best to learn, but he couldn't read "cat." I drilled him on the alphabet, tried to teach him the sounds that went with the letters. I don't remember if he ever learned anything, and I don't remember how many times we had to go into the cloakroom together, but it was more than twice.

One day as I was walking home after school, Ricky caught up to me and gave me a shove that sent me staggering. "You think you're better than me, don't you?"

My guts turned to slush. I tried to keep on walking just as though there was nothing happening, but there were four long blocks before I could run into our apartment and slam the door and be safe. "You think you're better than *everybody*, don't you?"

There was not a grown-up in sight. I knew that crying would doom me, so I willed myself not to cry. I kept thinking how unfair it was — me, the last kid in the world likely to believe that he was better than anybody else. "I don't think I'm better than you," I said. "I think we're all *equal*."

Ricky didn't say anything, but he didn't shove me again. I heard footsteps behind us and glanced back, saw that two more kids had joined us — Ricky's older brother and sister. If he was huge by first grade standards, they were gargantuan, and they were glaring at me. Now I knew what was happening. They'd planned it. They were going to jump me. Kids did that all the time, but I'd never thought it could happen to me.

"I think you're just as good as me," I said. "I think our teacher's mean. I hate her." He still didn't say anything.

It was like a scene in a comic book when one of the characters says to another, "You'd better talk fast," and I did. Nancy, the fast-talking girl who sat behind me in the first row, had nothing on me that day. I told Ricky the same things over and over — that I didn't think I was better than anybody else, that I thought we were all equal, that I hated being in the cloakroom just as much as he did, that it was *not fair*, that our teacher was *mean*, that she was an old witch, that everything in the first grade was lousy. I couldn't tell if he believed me or not. He wasn't saying a thing.

After we'd walked a couple more blocks to the sound of nothing but my voice, he said, "Are you my friend?"

"Yes," I said, astonished, "I'm your friend."

He held out his hand, and I took it. We shook on it. "He's my friend," he announced to his brother and sister, and then all three of them were smiling at me. I smiled back as best I could.

That was my first experience of having talked my way out of something, and, in matters of conflict resolution, it has remained my default position to this day. If somebody's firmly determined to get your ass, explaining yourself in enormous detail is not going to help you a bit — as I would find out later in life — but it's often worth a try, and it must have worked with Ricky. He came from the kind of West Virginia family that takes a vow of friendship seriously. For the rest of the school year, if anybody tried to pick on me, one of his huge red hands would appear out of nowhere to grab the offending kid by the shoulder or the scruff of the neck. "You let him alone," he'd say. "He's my friend."

## 3

I HATED SCHOOL. I learned so quickly from written material that I suffered the kind of tedious, interminable, bone-grinding boredom that can destroy your soul. I wasn't the only kid who was tortured in school. I remember a sad girl in the first grade. When called on, we had to stand up by the side of our desks, and then, when we were finished, we could sit down again. Whenever that little girl was called on, she stood up and promptly pissed herself. If you were a boy wearing pants, you had a slim chance of getting away with it — depending on how full your bladder was — but if you were a girl, you weren't allowed to wear pants, and if you were six, you were stuck in a skirt above your knees, and that left you nowhere to hide.

I used to pray, "Dear Lord, please don't let her wet herself again," but my prayers were never answered. Once she must have been holding it for a long time. An enormous flood went splashing down her bare legs. She hung her head in shame and sobbed, and the teacher got mad the way the teacher always did and sent her to the nurse's room. The janitor had to come and mop up the spot. The other kids called her "pissy pants." If school was a nightmare for me, it must have been worse for her. I don't know how she could have survived it. But like most things, it was just the way it was. No one ever took a kid's side on anything. Adults just said, "Oh, that's just life. You'll grow up and forget it." I've grown up, but I haven't forgotten it.

Somewhat later — it must have been in the third or fourth grade — we had to write letters and stand up in front of the classroom and read them. One of the girls had written what I thought was a very sweet letter to her girlfriend. It was filled with "dearest" and "darling" and "my beloved" and "my sweetheart" and many a fine flowery stock phrase from the valentines of the day. We saw a shudder of distaste pass across the teacher's face — a kind of *oh, yuck!* It wasn't right, the teacher said. It wasn't a good letter. It was too mushy. Good letters didn't have all that mushy stuff in them, and then I got it — the teacher had just made that girl ashamed of liking her friend. It was a terrible thing what the teacher had done, something she never should have done; it was wrong, it was mean, but I also knew that the teacher didn't intend it to be mean. She was just acting like a grown-up, and grown-ups were stupid.

One of my earliest memories of school is the day we had to draw scarecrows. The teacher had drawn her own version on the blackboard and labeled every part of it with the color she wanted us to use. She'd marked the hair on her scarecrow "black," but that didn't seem right to me. If you were actually making a scarecrow in your backyard, what black stuff could you possibly find to use for hair? The ones I'd seen had hair made out of straw, so I began to color my scarecrow's hair yellow.

Classrooms were as silent as dead zones in those days; if you talked, or even whispered, you were sent to the cloakroom, or worse, to the principal's office

71

where you might get paddled. I could hear the other kids breathing. I could hear the teacher's footsteps as she paced deliberately from desk to desk. I didn't dare to look up at her. I heard the teacher getting closer to me. I heard her shoes creaking. I heard her stop. She was looking down at my drawing. I was expecting her to be pleased; I was doing what they always told us to do — *I was thinking about it*. Maybe she'd even say, "Look at what Keith has done. He's the only one of you who remembered that scarecrows have hair made out of straw."

Her voice came out in a slow ugly hiss of wrenched-down fury. "I *said*, color the scarecrow's hair *black*."

I didn't even look up. I simply picked up my black crayon and began to color the scarecrow's hair black. She's wrong, I thought, and I'm right.

I knew that I'd never be allowed to explain why I'd chosen yellow. I knew that she was big and powerful and mean and I was just a little kid — that I couldn't possibly win — so I did what she'd ordered me to do, but I never lost my inner conviction. Like every other kid, I was forced into compliance, so I adopted the strategy of secret resistance. Yes, I thought, you can force me to obey your stupid rules, but inside I'll always know that I'm right and you're wrong. Eventually I'll grow big enough and old enough to understand how the world works, and then I'll do what I want, and you won't be able to stop me.

## 4

IN SCHOOL I BEGAN to have panic attacks — or something much like them. I'd never heard of anybody having scary things like that, so I didn't know what they were or that anybody else ever had them. They were yet another thing I didn't understand, and I took them as further proof that I was strange, utterly different from other children. Like night terrors, they made me ashamed; I called them "spells" and told no one about them, not even my mother or grandmother. I was sure that other children didn't have spells.

I would be sitting at my desk in school, or I'd be at the crafts table or looking for a book, and I'd feel the spell coming on like a buzzing at the back of my neck — then a nasty vibration like a wasp or a bee flying loose inside my mind, or even worse, many wasps or bees, a profound, ugly, rasping hum. If I paid any attention to it, I knew I'd start crying, or screaming, perhaps run out of the room or do something horrible and unforgivable, throw things on the floor or spit on someone. I absolutely couldn't do anything that would call attention to myself — not the slightest little thing — couldn't let anyone know that I was suffering from a spell that attacked me from the inside, *in my own mind*. I knew that it was a part of whatever was wrong with me — and there seemed to be plenty wrong with me — but I had to pretend to be a normal kid because my very life depended on it.

When the buzzing started, I'd be terrified because I knew I couldn't do anything about it and I might absolutely humiliate myself, disgrace myself, whimper or cry out. I knew I had to keep on doing whatever it was I was doing in a way that the teacher wouldn't notice me, that the other kids wouldn't notice me, even though the inside of my head was ringing more and more with thick nasty buzzing. I can remember getting too hot, that what I could see was narrowed down. There was a change in the light, a squeezing down in the light — things seemed to go yellow — and I had trouble breathing. My mother always told me, "If you're ever frightened, breathe slowly," so that was always the first thing I did. I taught myself to do it. I'd breathe as slowly as I could, and I'd tell myself things to make my mind go somewhere else. After I learned the multiplication tables, I used them as a charm, or a prayer, and they worked pretty well. If I recited the multiplication tables while the spell was going on, it stopped me from dwelling upon how horrible it was, how absolutely unendurable, so I'd chant silently in my mind: "Two times two is four, two times three is six, two times four is eight —"

BOYS FIGHT. I'd seen them doing it my whole life. I'd seen boys beat each other bloody. My mother always told me that it took more courage to walk away from a fight than it did to get into one. That didn't make a lot of sense to me — not even as much sense as what Jesus said when he told us to turn the other cheek. You might get the crap beaten out of you for turning the other cheek, but at least it was something you could do. Walking away from a fight was another matter. Sometimes you simply couldn't do that, and my mother should have known it. My grandmother knew it. She said, "Well, Keith, if you can't walk away, make sure you give as good as you get."

I did not get into fights. It wasn't that I was able to walk away from them; it was that whatever boys did to get into fights was not something that I did. But one day as I was walking up to school, another boy started something with me. I can't remember what it was, or how it began, but all of a sudden he was pushing me and I was pushing him — and he pushed me again and I pushed him back — and with that, we were well into it, committed to the standardized ritual that was the preliminary for a boys' fight in grade school. It wasn't as though we had anything against each other; we hardly knew each other. I remember the turning point, the unmistakable clarity of it. I could have walked away. It was almost time for school to start, and there would have been no disgrace in walking away — just stepping back and hurrying off to class — but something in me said, *no, not this time.* I wanted to fight.

Just as I'd seen happening with other boys, a ring of kids formed immediately around us, yelling, "Fight, fight, fight." I heard voices egging him on, voices egging me on. I was surprised that a group of girls from my class seemed to be making the most noise. "Hey, Keith's fighting," they yelled at each other. "Come on, Keith, go. Go.

Fight him. Go, go, go. Hit him, hit him, hit him." Their voices were high-pitched and thrilling.

He was bigger than I was, but nearly all the boys my age were bigger. He was not enormously bigger, but big enough that I shouldn't have been messing with him. I didn't care. Something bright and hot opened inside me that I hadn't known was in there, and I went after that boy in a fury — pushing him, pounding him, kicking him. My grandmother would have been proud of me. I was giving as good as I got. I was giving better than I got. I was a boy, and I wanted to hurt that other boy as much as I could, and I didn't care if he hurt me. I could not possibly lose — I would have died first. Then a teacher came out and stopped us, and we had to go in.

I was terrified that we'd be sent to the principal's office, but we weren't. I don't remember that boy's name, but I do remember that I didn't hold that fight against him and he didn't hold it against me. I'd wanted to fight to see if I could do it, to see what it felt like — and I'd done it. I'd learned that I could fight if I had to — and that fighting was mud-brained stupid. I never got into a fight again.

**5**

I'VE NEVER UNDERSTOOD the objection to reading as "an escape." Of course it's an escape and a damned good one. I read at night until my eyes burned and the book dropped out of my hands; the first thing I did when I woke up in the morning was reach over and pick it up.

Any book that was labeled "for girls," I was sure to read —
although sneakily, hiding the cover. I remember *Little
Women* and *The Secret Garden* and a stream of other
stories that blur together in my memory, the ongoing
adventures of spunky girls living in some long-gone
story-book past.

In those pre-television days, people read for pleasure,
and there were always books lying around our apartment. When I was in the second grade, I happened upon
Thorne Smith's *The Night Life of the Gods*. Of course I
didn't know who Thorne Smith was, and it didn't matter;
that book was the funniest thing I'd ever read in my
life. A mad scientist makes the statues of the Greek
gods and goddesses come alive, and they take off and
have goofy adventures in the present. Who were these
strange people? I needed to find out and began reading
Greek and Roman mythology. The Ohio County Public
Library — my favorite place in all of Wheeling — had
some books on mythology for kids, and I read those.
Then I moved on to grown-up books. Within a year or
two I had read every book on Greek and Roman mythology in our library.

I read big, thick, impossible books with millions
and millions of words that I didn't understand, and I
read madly as fast as I could, jumping in over my head
and floundering in the words. Sometimes I'd sound out
the big words and try to remember them; other times I
just skipped right over them. I knew those books were
way too hard for me, but I didn't care. I forced myself

to keep swimming into that resistant density — words, words, words — because there was something I knew I had to get. Pretty soon I had the world of Olympus, the whole pantheon of the gods and goddesses with both their Greek and Roman names, parading around in my head.

The story of Tiresias made a big impression on me. Here's pretty much the way I construed it when I was in grade school. Tiresias was out for a walk one day when he saw two snakes twined around each other, and Z A P, he was turned into a girl. He lived as a girl for a while, and then he saw those same two snakes again, and Z A P, he was turned back into a boy.

One night they were having an argument up on Mount Olympus. The Greek gods and goddesses argued all the time up there. Zeus, the king of the gods, said that girls had more fun, but Hera, his wife, the queen of the gods, said no, that wasn't true, boys had more fun. Somebody said, "Hey, Tiresias has been both a boy and a girl. Let's ask him," so they sent for Tiresias. He came up to Mount Olympus, and they put the question to him. He said, "Girls have more fun."

Hera was so angry that he'd told the truth — she'd wanted to keep it a secret — that she struck him blind. Well, one god can never undo what another god has done, so Zeus couldn't do anything about that, but he felt sorry for Tiresias, so he gave him a different kind of sight. He made it so he could see with his mind — so he could see into the future.

That was one of the stories I wished was real because then maybe I'd be able to switch back and forth between being a boy and being a girl. By then I was pretty sure that I was a boy — although I didn't know exactly why or how — but I kept thinking that maybe it was a mistake. I knew that I wasn't a *real* boy, and I also knew that I couldn't ever admit that to anyone. So maybe I should have been a girl — or maybe, just as I had always suspected, I was a girl in disguise — but if I got a chance to be a girl for real, then I'd know whether girls had more fun or not.

BOYS IN SCOTLAND wear kilts so of course I discovered my Scots heritage — although, to connect myself to the McCoys, I had to go back and sideways for several generations — and I had my grandmother make me a Scots outfit in the girls' plaid, Royal Stewart. The kilt looked exactly the way I wanted it to — like a pleated skirt that any of the girls I knew might have worn. I often changed into it when I came home from school, but I never would have worn it outside. Then my mother suggested that we visit my girl cousins who lived in Martins Ferry. They had a Scots heritage too.

I'm amazed at myself now that I had the courage to do it. While we were riding the bus, I was so sick with dread that the entire world was buzzing just like it did when I had spells, but none of the grown-ups paid any attention to me. They must have seen me as nothing remarkable, just a little kid in a skirt. When we got to my cousins' house, they didn't seem the least bit surprised to see me in a skirt either. After I made my obligatory speech about my Scots heritage, none of us mentioned it again. I wish I could remember details of that night, but I can't. I was surprised at how well we got along, how easily we played together. Playing girls' games with three girls while wearing a skirt felt absolutely right to me — as though I had, for one magical night, been welcomed onto the girls' team. Yes, I thought, girls did have more fun.

## 6

WHEN I WAS IN the second grade, my mother asked me if I wanted to take tap dance lessons. As we often did after dinner, we were talking in the kitchen, and I still have brightly colored flashes of that conversation playing on the screen in my mind. My mother was standing at the sink drying the dishes; too antsy to sit in a chair and talk like a grown-up, I was pacing back and forth. Her question made me immediately suspicious. I knew that dance lessons were for girls. "I don't know," I said.

It was a good thing for a man to be able to dance, she told me. Men who were good dancers were lots of fun and well liked. She had never told me that my father was a tap dancer — she wouldn't say a word about it for years — but I felt his presence nonetheless. *Oh*, I thought, *she wants to make me like my father.*

I didn't want to be like my father — that faceless guy who had vanished and never written me a single letter — and I especially didn't want to be like my father if that's what my mother wanted. I could sense the movie playing in her mind, and I didn't want to be cast for any role in it, certainly not as *the good dancer who's lots of fun*. But she talked on and on about it, and she must have worn me down because I reluctantly agreed. Sure, I would try out tap dancing lessons, why not?

There's a distinctive smell to dance schools that's hard to describe, but anyone who's ever walked into one will recognize it at once. Forget any notion that little girls are clean, neat, and immaculate as angels. Begin with the smell of dancewear the girls have been carrying around unwashed for days, then add soggy wet wool that's been left to dry on a radiator, and the dry odor of the bare wood of the studio floors, the vinegar used to polish the mirrors, the perfumes and powders worn by the moms and the teachers, and it all blends into a bouquet — sweetish and soiled — that says "dance school." That smell would lodge itself in my mind and wait patiently for me to find it when I would walk with my younger daughter into her first dance school.

My mother and I had to walk up a long flight of stairs, so, as I left the street, I was leaving behind the ordinary world, entering into another — one as outlandish as any story-book castle. The windows looked down on the street — were high, high, high above the street — and off to the left was an area that looked like somebody's attic; the ceiling sloped down at a sharp diagonal, and sitting on a floor there, under the eaves, was a cluster of girls older than I was. They had their books and schoolwork spread out around them, were whispering to each other; they were all wearing pink tights and pink ballet slippers. We passed a studio where other girls, even older, were holding onto a wooden bar; I saw them multiplied in huge mirrors — girls in shiny pink slippers who were balancing on the very tips of their toes like the girls I'd seen on the stage. It was the most girlish place I'd ever been in my life. Not on that day — and never once on any of the other days when I went back there — did I ever see a single boy.

My mother had to talk to a grown-up lady. There was a complex negotiation going on between them that had to do with money, and I didn't try to follow it, but then the grown-up lady said that, yes, they did have a class for boys, and I started to pay attention. I couldn't go into that class yet, she said. They were way far ahead of me, and I'd have to catch up. So I could either take private lessons or go into a class with girls who were beginners like me.

I felt the same sense of inevitability I'd had when I'd been seated with girls at school — *of course* I'd be put into a class with girls — but my mother surprised me by saying, no, she didn't think that would be a good idea. I should probably take private lessons. I was both relieved and disappointed.

The next order of business was tap shoes. The grown-up lady measured my feet. I was, as I knew perfectly well, *delicate*, and so I had tiny feet. They did sell boys'

82

tap shoes, but I was a year or two away from being able to wear them, so the grown-up lady suggested that I could wear girls' tap shoes while I was learning — just until my feet got big enough — and took a pair out of a box and showed them to me and my mother. She actually wanted me to try them on. Now I was truly alarmed. They weren't going to fool me. It didn't matter what those shoes were called. Even if they had taps on them, they were black patent party shoes like Arlene wore to church, and they were exactly what the tap boys had been wearing on the stage — those boys who'd been pretending to be girls. "What do you think?" my mother asked me. I desperately wanted them and wouldn't have worn them under pain of death.

Somebody might as well have thrown a ball at me. I already knew that I couldn't catch it; if it was going to hit me, it was going to hit me. Maybe I could duck out of the way, or maybe not, but the best thing for me to do was not say anything, not show anything, not do anything at all, so that whatever happened would be *somebody's else's fault, not my fault.* "Well, Keith," my mother said again, "what do you think?"

I didn't even look at her.

"If he's got an old pair of oxfords," the grown-up lady said, "you could take them to the shoe man, and he could put taps on them."

I don't remember how many tap lessons I took — several. They assigned me to a girl, probably a high-school kid, but to me she seemed enormously grown up. I had to go into a room alone with her and shut the door. She was wearing pretty black patent tap shoes, and I was wearing an old ugly pair of my own shoes with taps screwed onto them. We would stand face to face, and then she would go, tappaty tappaty tappaty tap, "Now you do it." I knew almost at once that I couldn't do it.

I would find out later that the only way I can learn anything that involves physical activity is if the movement is broken into small, discrete units — okay, first you do this, and then you do this, and then you do this — so I can practice each unit independently, step-by-step, and eventually put it all together. That's the way I would be taught to shoot a rifle in military school, and that's why I would turn out to be a good shot. But watching somebody's feet go tappaty tappaty tappaty tap and then trying to imitate them was impossible for me. She'd say, "That's not too bad. Try it again," and I'd try it again, and she'd say to my mother afterward, "Oh, he'll pick it up," but I knew that I would never pick it up. I had no assurance that I was doing anything right, and without that assurance, I couldn't proceed. If I'd had a different kind of teacher, I might have learned to tap — or maybe not. The dance school both fascinated and repelled me. I loved the feminine all-girl atmosphere, but I couldn't relax in there. I might be like a girl, but I wasn't a real girl. Eventually I convinced my mother that tap was not for me. I was enormously relieved — and then spent years feeling that I had missed out on something.

MY AUNT ELEANOR — Billy and Becky's mom — died on the Fourth of July. That nice gentle woman, my favorite aunt, had got cancer in her leg. It had appeared first as a bruise, and the grown-ups seemed to think the bruise had caused it, so, for years afterward, I was careful not to bump into things because I didn't want to give myself cancer.

My cousin Billy had always been a problem kid, and his mother's illness and then, later on, her death seemed to make him worse. Many of his escapades had already become family legends. When he was little, he had sleep-walked regularly and one night had wandered out of his bedroom and peed through the banister down into the front hall. After he got older, things had a nasty habit of bursting into flames whenever he was around. I don't know how many fires he set, but the curtains in the living room was the one that people remembered and talked about.

One night when Eleanor was in the hospital, they had to leave Billy alone, and he threw an entire dozen eggs down the basement stairs. As the story went, he'd done it deliberately, carefully, one egg at a time. The eggs went splat on the water heater at the bottom of the stairs, turned it into an omelet, and it had cost my uncle Bill a fortune to get it fixed. That's the way the story was always told, and it wasn't until years later that it occurred to me to ask an obvious question. It must have been terrible when Billy's mom was dying of cancer, but why on earth had they left a six-year-old in the house alone?

I have a small flash of memory so elusive that I can't decide whether it's real or I made it up — Billy opening his hand to show me a pack of matches. The legends about him were repeated endlessly. The minute Billy saw matches, they vanished. They had to watch him all the time. They had to go through his clothes, go through his room. What he really wanted — he told me this — was a lighter, one of those metal Zippos that went click. I'd never been allowed to play with matches, but Billy showed me how easy they were to light. He could light my mother's Zippo too, just as quick as a wink. He knew that you filled a Zippo with lighter fluid, and he knew that if you squirted lighter fluid on something, it burned really fast.

Billy's mom got cancer so bad that she had to have her leg amputated. My mom and I visited her right afterward. I remember Eleanor in bed with only one leg, and I tried not to look because I knew it was impolite to stare. The part of the covers where a leg should have been was flat as a pancake, and that saddened and alarmed me. But Eleanor was nice the way she always was. She was even cheerful, and I thought she was very brave. I was also there visiting when a man came around and explained to her how to walk with a false leg. It had a spring mechanism in it, and if you adjusted your body in a certain way, the leg sprang forward. She walked around on that false leg for a while, but then she died.

Aunt Eleanor was the first dead person I ever saw. She was at Kepner's Funeral Home, and I was afraid to look at her, but my mother said it was okay, took my hand and led me over to the coffin. We looked at our people for the last time out of respect, she said. We did it so we could remember them, say goodbye. There were so many flowers the smell was making me sick. Everybody said how pretty Eleanor looked, and it was true, but I didn't know why it should matter if you're pretty when you're dead. She didn't look like what I'd expected a dead person to look like. She didn't look asleep. I never would have thought she was asleep. She was still impossibly blonde, and they'd put so much makeup on her she looked like a painted doll, and I thought, oh, that's probably what it must be like — to be dead and to be made pretty so you can be buried and look like that forever. I wouldn't have touched her for anything.

"She's not there anymore," my mother told me. "That's only her body. She's gone to be with God."

Eleanor was a beautiful lady and had always been kind to me. I knew I was supposed to talk to Becky and Billy, say something nice to them, but I was too embarrassed and ashamed. It was their mother who'd died, and I didn't know what to say. I felt bad, but you couldn't just go up to somebody and say, "I feel bad," when you knew they felt worse than you did because it was their mother. I wouldn't talk to them. I purposefully avoided them. "I want to go home," I said. The flowers really stunk; it was the worst smell in the world.

IT WASN'T UNTIL my uncle Bill was long dead before my mother told me how much she had resented him. He was a gambler and a drunk, she told me, and he'd lost Eleanor's insurance money in a poker game so my mother had to pay for the funeral. Bill had always been a drinker, but after Eleanor died, he took up the passionate, single-minded, and deeply committed drinking that would kill him in his fifties.

Surely I must have pasted other things than pictures of girls into my scrapbooks — although that's all I remember — but my cousin Billy pasted pictures of whiskey bottles into his. We were both collectors. Just as I wanted to see how many pictures of cute girls I could collect, Billy wanted to see how many pictures of Four Roses whiskey he could collect. That was his dad's favorite.

**8**

IN THE THIRD GRADE I decided to go to school on Halloween as a girl. I knew by then that I was very different from other kids — not just in boy-girl stuff but in all kinds of ways — but everybody took me for a boy and expected me to act like one, and I'd been doing my best. I'd stopped wearing my kilt and had not allowed myself to wear anything else even remotely girlish, so being a girl for Halloween was a huge and daring reversal for me. I think now that I wanted to do it for the same reason I'd wanted to get into a fight — to see if I could, to see what it felt like.

I knew exactly what I was doing. The rules of Halloween were simple and known to everyone — you could be anything you wanted, but you didn't want people to keep asking, "Who are you supposed to be?" so you had to be a character everybody would know at first glance. Esmeralda, the Gypsy girl, fit the bill. I knew her from the *Classic Comics* version of *The Hunchback of Notre Dame* and so did a lot of other kids. My mother and grandmother knew her from the old silent movie that had starred Lon Chaney as Quasimodo, so re-creating Esmeralda's costume was not a problem for them.

I wanted a wig, but my mother talked me into a "fall." I'd never heard of one before, but she explained that it was false hair attached to your real hair to make it seem longer. She found one that looked like human hair and even matched the color of my own hair; I wore it in two long braids bobby-pinned down and held in place with a bandana. I can't remember if my grandmother made the peasant blouse or we bought it — I think it was cotton and white — but I was much more interested in the skirt and watched her making it on the sewing machine. She used a cheap, shiny synthetic fabric — brilliantly colored with vertical stripes, gaudy enough to say "Gypsy" loud and clear. Like Esmeralda's in the comic book, it fell to just above my ankles. My grandmother put rouge and lipstick on me, several strings of beads, and clip-on bangle earrings that distracted and irritated me until my earlobes went numb enough to allow me to forget that I was wearing them. The costume wouldn't have felt real without girl's shoes, and I borrowed a pair of party shoes from Arlene. The sensation of wearing them sticks clearly in my mind. Compared to boys' shoes, they seemed light as feathers; their soles were so thin that I could feel the bricks in the sidewalk.

It seems appropriate to me now that I chose the Gypsies — not the real ones, about whom neither I nor anybody else knew anything at all, but the stereotype of the Gypsies, one of our versions of "the other," those shadowy folk who provide us with a screen for our projected fears and fascinations, who live on the margins and don't play by the rules. When I was a child, there were things that everyone "knew" about the Gypsies — they didn't have a home of their own but wandered all over the earth, always distrusted, never settling down anywhere; they knew magic, could tell fortunes; they stole children and they might steal me. I knew that things like that didn't happen in real life, but it made a good story to tell myself.

I was excited when I was dressed as Esmeralda, but I wasn't the least bit nervous. It was Halloween, after all, and I expected everyone to play by the rules, and everyone did — although I had a scary moment when I met Ricky dressed as Frankenstein's monster. The moment I saw him, I thought it was the perfect costume for him — that it suited him just as much as mine suited me — but if anybody was going to make fun of me or give me a hard time, Ricky as a monster was the kid most likely to do it. He surprised me by saying, "Hey, Keith, you look real pretty."

I said what my mother had always told me to say when you get a compliment: "Thank you."

So I entered our third grade classroom escorted by Frankenstein's monster, ushered in with all the gallantry he must have learned from the movies — aping the mannerisms of a solicitous gentleman with a young lady — and I deeply appreciated him for it. A lot of the girls told me I looked pretty too.

I made no effort to pretend to be a girl, didn't try to change the way I walked or talked or moved, didn't try to imitate any of the sugar-and-spice cuteness I'd seen the tap boys doing. I didn't feel the need to do anything special. I played Esmeralda as myself.

I remember a tension at first — a diffuse misalignment of social energies — and then I remember it melting away. After about an hour, everything felt absolutely normal — except for the fact that we were all in costume. We were no longer seated by grades, so my regular seat wasn't with the girls any more, but when we were split into girls' and boys' activities, I joined the girls without a moment's hesitation, and no one seemed to mind, or even notice, not even the teacher. I joined the girls at recess too — something I never would have done as a boy. The girls had known me since the first grade and included me automatically in their group as though I'd always been there.

Near the end of the school day we were paraded in front of the class, one at a time, so we could get a good look at each other, and then all of us voted for various categories. I won "prettiest costume." Of course I was pleased. My mother, grandmother, and I had put a lot of work into that costume, and I too thought that it was the prettiest costume in the third grade. I felt honored and vindicated.

My successful public appearance as a girl left me with a lot to think about, and I've thought about it ever since. As with other significant experiences from my childhood, I can't tell now what's my original memory and what's my rehashing of it, so this is the best I can do. By the end of that day I knew how easy it would be for me — how absolutely natural — to be a girl. At five, or even at six, I might have taken the experience as proof that I really *was* a girl; at nearly nine, there was no way I could have thought that. I still didn't know the crucial difference between boys and girls, but I did know that it had to be more obvious than something deep inside you couldn't see, and no matter how right I'd felt being a girl with other girls, I knew that on Halloween I hadn't been a real girl.

### 9

BY NINE, I was well on my way to becoming a solitary and isolated kid. I'd become too old to play with girls, and both they and I knew it. I played with my cousins, and with other boys sometimes — pretending to be a boy like them — but I had no real friends, and the characters I was meeting in books were more important to me than real people. My mother had always encouraged me to read anything I wanted. One of her friends was a librarian who let me roam around at will — even into the adult section. I'd pick any book at all, give it to my mother, and she'd check it out.

I'd been reading science fiction since I'd been six, and I'd go on reading it all through high school. I hardly ever remembered the name of the authors, but I remembered *the stories* — or at least bits and pieces of them, glittering now in a vast retrospective display at the back of my head that looks like a sky-sized cover of *Galaxy Magazine* — striped planets with multiple moons flung out among impossibly distant stars.

Of course I loved the alien worlds, and the gadgets — the deep-space rockets, the cars that transformed into airplanes, the tiny radio devices embedded behind our ears that put us in constant touch with the collective knowledge of all humanity, the ray guns that vaporized our enemies and left behind for a moment the after-image of running feet — but I loved the weird ideas even more. A cell divides in time rather than in space, and a woman becomes her own daughter. The visitors from some unknown galaxy first announce their presence on earth by curing everyone of cancer. The people on a distant planet look just like us but change their sex every six months. Connected by telepathy, strangely dissimilar beings form symbiotic units. In ecstatic fusion, an isolated hero is absorbed into cosmic consciousness. Alien life forms can be anything, can be murderous or benign, can be built of something other than boring, predictable carbon rings. Whole other worlds with their own laws and peculiarities exist side by side with our ordinary one. We can travel for years at speeds faster than light to arrive right back where we started or get sucked into black holes to bubble up somewhere else so far away it can't be described in terms of either time or space. There are intelligences so superior to ours that we seem like little more than clever monkeys in comparison, realities so different from ours that the terms "life" and "death" have no meaning.

Reading science fiction was one of the most valuable things I did as a child. It shifted the center of the universe away from the human, made me skeptical of all human claims to truth. I had no doubt that there were other intelligences in the universe — with their own viewpoints, larger and stranger than ours. At a time when it appeared that nothing could ever be anything other than what it was, science fiction gave me a sense of infinite possibilities.

ONE EVENING as I was wandering through the stacks in the library, I saw a book called *Man and Superman*. Oh, I thought, I bet I'll like that one. A real grown-up book about Superman was bound to be much more interesting than a comic book. When I got it home, I discovered that it wasn't about Superman, the guy with the cape.

It was a play, and I couldn't figure out what on earth it was about. I'd never read a play before, but it was easy, just people talking, and when they were moving around or doing something, the play told you all about it. The people talked a lot — boy, did they ever talk a lot! It drew me right in — I especially liked it when everybody went to Hell — and I read the whole thing. I never did get the point of the story, but I made sure to remember the name of the man who wrote it — Bernard Shaw.

But there were two plays in that book. The second was *Saint Joan*, and that one really got to me. I'd been able to tell that there were things in *Man and Superman* that were meant to be funny, or light, or — I'm not sure how I would have put it — satirical, but there was nothing like that in *Saint Joan*. It was deadly serious. I already knew what a saint was, or I was pretty sure I did — from the Bible, from Sunday school, and from hymns. There was the Doxology that we sang every Sunday which has the line, "All the saints adore thee, casting down their golden crowns around a glassy sea" — a line that gave me pause as a child, and a line that gives me pause today. There were saints in the stained-glass windows too. I liked Saint Michael because he looked like a girl with armor on. He prepared me for Saint Joan, for imagining what she must have looked like.

Right from the start I had problems with Christianity. God the Father is not a useful metaphor to offer a child who has no father, and God in that guise felt exactly like my father — infinitely distant, utterly silent, and not in the least concerned about me. I did a little better with Jesus, but not much; he was *a man*, after all, and not only that, he was a man who had a close relationship with *his father*. I read about Jesus in the good old King James, and I could never understand why people called him "gentle." He had his gentle moments, but he could just as easily be mean and scary. The only part of the Holy Trinity that appealed to me was the science fiction part — the Holy Ghost. But I always liked the idea of saints.

Saints were, the best that I could tell, not simply people who did God's will — anybody could do that; even *I* could do that — but people who were in direct contact with God, or with other saints or layers of heavenly beings, or, as in a science fiction story, with superior entities. Saints were people who had the energy of God flowing through them and into the world. It was like the story of Jesus as he's walking through the streets, and the woman touches his garment. He says, "Who touched me?" and he knows that *someone* touched him because he'd felt the power go out of him. That was the kind of power I thought flowed through saints and connected them with God, and with the heavenly host who would be, at the end of time — or perhaps were at that very moment — casting down their golden crowns around a glassy sea.

So *Saint Joan* was on the same level as the Bible. It was not fun, was not meant to be fun, was as serious as you could get. It was about *a saint*. She was a "maid" — a girl — but she dressed up like a boy, led whole armies, won battles, and turned a weak little creep into the King of France. As often happens to saints, the stupid, thick-headed authorities burned her at the stake — just as ignorant Earthlings often hurt or reject benign visitors from other planets. Knowing myself, I'm guessing that I must have cried when they burned her, although I have no memory of doing it. I do remember feeling the full horror of her ghastly death. I'd burned myself by accident a few times, so I knew what fire felt like for only a second, and I tried to imagine what it must be like to be tied to a stake and have the fire lit under you, to feel it getting closer and closer, and then what it must be like to feel it burn up your toes and know that it was just getting started. It made me so sick at my stomach I couldn't think about it for very long. It was not lost on me that Joan of Arc had been burned up for acting like a boy. She was the first of the tomboy warrior girls who would fascinate me for the rest of my life. Her story marked me so deeply it's as though I'd always known it. I loved her with all my heart. If I'd been a Catholic boy, I would have prayed to her.

### 10

AFTER AUNT ELEANOR DIED, my uncle Bill and my cousins had to move into a small apartment on the south end of the Island, and all manner of strange things from Bill's house began to flow over to our house. We had moved farther up Front Street so my grandmother could take care of her ancient aunt, Keziah Berdelia Lippincott Brown, known to us as "Aunt Deal." Compared to our safe little apartment, our new house seemed enormous and scary to me. It even had an attic that we stuffed with our junk, so now another layer of Uncle Bill's junk got added. We were pack rats. You never could tell when something might come in handy. There were lots of interesting and mysterious things up there in the attic, and I wanted to see what.

I found a big, thick, dusty, brown medical book up there. It had anatomical drawings as clear as anything. It had drawings of a man with a penis and testicles, a woman with a vagina. The book made me sick — dizzy and sweaty, afraid that I was going to faint or throw up — but I kept sneaking back up to the attic to study the chapter on human reproduction. I learned what men and women looked like naked, what they had hidden inside them, and what all that stuff was for. I didn't like any of it, but I knew that it had to be true. I'd wanted to know how I could be *absolutely sure* whether I was a boy or a girl, and now I knew.

I was furious with my mother. She had lied to me. "Their bodies are different," she'd said. In those precise drawings I could see that, yes, their bodies *were* different — and, yes, some of the things that were different were deep inside, but there were also things that were different on *the outside*, things that anybody could see. My mother had told me the sneakiest, most underhanded lie there is — the kind of lie when you tell something that's true *but you leave out the important part.*

## 11

I KEPT TRYING to find ways to be more like a boy. There were certain skills I'd never learned, things that other boys learned from their fathers, and it finally dawned on me that I didn't need a father to teach them to me. Our neighbors had a son who was home on leave. He was everything I thought a young man ought to be — lean and tall, muscular, with thick chest hair and a big lazy grin — a sailor home from the sea. I walked up the street and asked him if he would teach me how to ride a bike.

I inherited my first bike from my cousin, Becky — a boy's bike, an old blue Schwinn with a back-pedal brake that screamed like a banshee. Once I got the hang of it, I was amazed and annoyed at myself that it had taken me so long to overcome my fear — riding a bike felt as easy and natural as breathing. I could ride from our apartment all the way down to the south end, around the loop by the Downs, and back again before I had time to think about it. I rode it for hours — not going anywhere, not stopping to talk to anybody, just riding.

By the time I was going into the fifth grade, I still hadn't made a single close friend. I went to school and did enough of whatever they required of me so I wouldn't get into trouble, and then I went home and read whatever book I had going at the moment, and if I was feeling antsy, I rode my bike. The kids in my class had stopped being real for me. Even though I'd been going to school with them since I was six, I sometimes couldn't remember their names or even tell them apart.

Summer day camp was a different matter. There you had to interact with other kids whether you wanted to or not, and we were, of course, divided into same-sex groups. I'd learned to imitate other boys well enough by then so that I could fit in reasonably well. Even though I still hated playing ball, I pretended it was okay because there was no way I could get out of it — and then one day I discovered the bunt. When I'd been forced to play ball as a little kid, the boys would yell at me, "Hit it, hit it, hit it." If you can't see the ball coming, it's unlikely you're going to hit it, but after I started wearing glasses in the third grade, I could see it just fine. I didn't have much power, but there was nothing wrong with my eye-hand coordination, and I discovered that it wasn't too hard — in fact, with a slow pitcher, it was almost easy — to wait until the ball was just over the plate and then, at the very last minute, to interrupt its flight so it popped off my bat with a satisfying little click.

The other boys who'd been used to playing sandlot baseball in which the main thing a boy wanted to do was slam the son-of-a-gun a million miles into the stratosphere were completely flummoxed by the bunt, were never ready for it, and I could usually make it to first base. I still couldn't throw or catch worth a shit, but I'd gone from being an utter liability on the team to being a small asset, and I was no longer the last kid to get chosen.

It was the first social success I'd ever had as a boy, and I was proud of myself.

I had another skill that gave me status in summer camp — my ability to tell stories. I made up long fabulous tall tales that I told the other boys as we rode back and forth on the bus or ate our lunches. When we met at the bus stop in the morning, they'd say, "Start telling," and I would. I had a live audience right in front of me, so I was learning essential things about storytelling — the use of pacing, vivid details, cliff-hangers — the beginnings of those skills I'd need later when I began writing my stories down on paper. Day camp was friendly enough, and I liked those other boys well enough, and they seemed to like me, but I was constantly aware of being in disguise.

My cousin Billy was the closest thing I had to a friend. We'd paired up at family gatherings ever since we'd been little. He was a year younger than I was, and I'd always felt that age difference, but over the years we'd grown into an unspoken pact — we could always rely on each other. We called each other up every few days and chatted about nothing much. Every week or two we walked over to town and went to a movie. We did talk, but in the circumscribed way that boys talked, carefully avoiding anything to do with feelings. I never told him about my inner turmoil just as he never told me what it was like to have his mother die when he'd been seven, but we knew each other pretty well nonetheless. We hadn't chosen each other the way friends do; we'd simply been born into the same family. He was my old pal, my sidekick, *my cousin*.

## 12

UNCLE BILL GOT A JOB as a night clerk somewhere down the river, and my cousins Billy and Becky moved in with us. That was okay with me; I liked my cousins. Every week or two my mother took Billy and me to a movie. Afterward we'd walk down to the Twelfth Street Newsstand where they sold a million magazines. Some weren't for kids — like the trash Uncle Bill read — but I loved seeing those forbidden ladies with their bright red lips and come-on eyes staring down at me from their glossy covers. There were magazines for girls too, like the ones Becky bought; I flipped through them secretly. And every month I bought three magazines, read them cover to cover, and stored them on my bookshelves because *I was collecting them — Galaxy, Fantasy and Science Fiction,* and *Dance Magazine.*

I hadn't seen dance on the stage since my aunt Eleanor had taken me and Billy to that recital where I'd seen the tap boys pretending to be girls, but in *Dance Magazine* I read about great performances in New York and Los Angeles and San Francisco — distant dream cities where I knew I would go someday. I read all the articles on technique and learned what some of the terms meant; they were in French, my father's language — *port de bras, en l'air, rond de jambe, pointe* and *demi-pointe.* I'd loved ballet girls ever since I'd first seen them; now I taped their pictures to my walls — girls in tutus, girls on pointe — and drew or painted my own versions of them.

If my mother thought that a magazine for young dancers was an odd thing for me to be reading, or that pictures of ballerinas were inappropriate for a boy's bedroom, she never said so.

Everything I thought or felt had another side to it. "Ambivalent" is not the right word, not strong enough, implying, as it does, an inability to choose one side or the other. I could, depending upon the mood I was in, hold opinions that were diametrically opposed to each other, and hold them with fiery conviction. Sometimes I was bitterly disappointed that I hadn't made more of an effort to learn by the tappaty-tappaty-tap-now-you-do-it method. I should have been — badly wanted to be — a dancer, and the thought of being surrounded by pink-clad ballet girls was close to my idea of heaven. Then, at other times, the demonic toggle switch in my mind would flip over and I would congratulate myself on how sneakily I'd fooled my mother, and everybody else, by pretending that I couldn't learn to tap. Whew, what a close call! I would rather have died than go to dance school. Boys who took dance lessons were sissies.

I'd always hated the word "sissy," but it had by then taken on a terrible emotional charge. It was the most foul, filthy, and degrading name I could imagine, so vile it stopped my thought processes dead. "Like a girl" was okay; I had never minded that being said about me — well, that depended on who said it and how it was said — but girls were smarter than boys, could read better, draw better, talk to grown-ups better, do a lot of things better. And then there was something else that I couldn't define; it didn't have anything to do with who was better at what. Girls were girls — that's all there was to it. I was and always had been like a girl, and when my mental switch was flipped in that direction, I was still proud of it and wanted to join the girls' team and do the things they did. But when my mental switch was set on boy, I was terrified of crossing the deadly line into sissy.

Terrified or not, I kept pushing the line. During my first few years of school, I had obsessively avoided anything the least bit girlish — well, except for discovering my Scots heritage — but gradually I started doing just the opposite. My friends were people in books, and I didn't care what real kids thought of me — well, I *almost* didn't care. Except for large-ticket items like suits, I was allowed to buy my own clothes, so I played a dangerous game in which I tried to see how much I could make myself look like a girl without actually wearing a single article of girls' clothing.

I still liked the clear nail polish my grandmother used to put on me. Although it was far from common, grown men sometimes wore it, and that gave me permission, so I wore it so much of the time I forgot I was wearing it. In the '50s they hardly ever sold any articles of clothing that were what we would now call "gender neutral," but whenever they did, I was sure to find them — like saddle shoes or penny loafers that were exactly the same for both boys and girls. I sometimes wore them with shorts and knee socks like a girl — although never to school. When my mental switch flipped back to boy, I was ashamed of myself and vowed to stop dressing like that. Then, a week or so later, the switch would go the other way and I'd be doing it again. I couldn't trust myself — couldn't find any single consistent reliable position — and that gave me an awful sickening feeling.

It seems remarkable to me now, but except for that ghastly ordeal when those no-good boys had trapped Arlene and me in the storage locker, I was never badly picked on or bullied. I'd been called a sissy when I'd been little, but as I got older, kids stopped calling me that — although there were times when I must have looked like a sissy and they must surely have noticed — or maybe that's not how they read me. No matter how much I think about it now, I can't make any conclusive sense of this, so the best I can offer are a few guesses. Everybody on the Island knew everybody else, and I'd always been like a girl, and everybody knew that. Maybe the kids had simply got used to me — or I might have been saved by being weird in other ways. I was the brain, the egghead who could name all the planets and describe them in detail, who could talk about galaxies, dwarf stars, deep space, and the speed of light. The other kids might have seen me not so much as girlish as simply alien — and possibly even interesting and exotic. I don't remember any hostility coming from kids my own age. When they wanted to tease me, they didn't call me "sissy," they called me "space cadet."

# part III

# A MAN'S WORK

**1**

SCHOOL HAD GONE from being hell to being tolerable. I might have made no friends, but I'd made no enemies either. A boy doesn't show up dressed as a girl on Halloween and get himself elected "prettiest" if the other kids haven't got used to him, if they don't, on some level, like him. Because I'd always been there, a space must have been created for me so I could go on being there — which is how we do things in West Virginia. Our teachers tested us constantly, and I always got high scores on everything, so they must have been cutting me a lot of slack. Then, all of a sudden, things were different. In the fifth grade I got Sarah Brokaw as my homeroom teacher, and she cut me no slack at all. I may have forgotten all of my other teachers, but I have no trouble remembering Miss Brokaw.

If you had gone to Central Casting and said, "I'm looking for a stereotype of the nasty, old maid school teacher . . . a flat, one-dimensional, cardboard cut-out character with no redeeming qualities . . . an old bitch straight from hell," they would have sent you Miss Brokaw.

When she walked in the door, we rose instantly to our feet and chanted in unison, "Good morning, Miss Brokaw." Then we sat down just as quickly and folded our hands on the tops of our desks. Not a word, not a whisper, not a sigh was tolerated. Needless to say, both the insides and outsides of our desks were neatness exemplified, and no ink smudges were ever to be seen on our written work. Miss Brokaw spoke in a voice as vigorously projected as an actor's — articulating every syllable, snapping out every consonant. She specialized in that ancient, tried-and-true pedagogical device — scathing sarcasm. With a few well-chosen words, she could reduce even the most self-assured of us to a status somewhat lower than stepped-on dog shit. Miss Brokaw was a woman who could not possibly — not even for a few seconds, not even once in her life — have ever liked a child.

Always before, my teachers had let me read pretty much anything I'd wanted, but Miss Brokaw told me that I was required to read the books on the fifth-grade list. I told her — politely — that those books were too easy for me. She accused me of "open defiance." This conversation was taking place in the usual utter silence of our classroom, with me standing and all the other kids sitting, their hands folded neatly on their desks in front of them. I hadn't intended anything remotely like open defiance, but reading was sacred to me, and no one before had ever told me what to read. It didn't make any sense for me to read books at the fifth-grade level when one of the tests I'd taken had said that I was reading at the senior high level — and I told her that. She said, "I can see that it is going to take constant daily punishment to make you obey."

Her eyes were burning straight into mine. She's not just mean, I thought, she's evil. She's not just bad or wrong or stupid or nasty, she's evil the way the Bible means evil. "You are going to read the fifth-grade books," she said.

I said nothing and intended to go on saying nothing no matter how long I had to stand there. I knew better than to say to her what I'd just said to myself — "No, I'm not."

What did "constant daily punishment" mean? Was she going to make me stand in the cloakroom the way they did to kids in the first grade? Was she going to keep me in at recess and after school? Was she going to send me to the principal's office? Were there other strange, cruel, and unusual things she was going to dream up — punishments I couldn't even imagine? I felt the same sense of sickening inevitability in the face of disaster that I'd always felt, but, as usual, there didn't seem to be anything I could do about it.

LOTS OF HEAVY THINGS came down on me in the fifth grade — it was a pivotal year. That was when Christine Jorgensen hit the newspapers. I was fascinated by Christine, knew that her story was of vital importance to me, and read every article or news item about her I could find — read secretly, hiding myself behind the racks in the Twelfth Street Newsstand. If you Google her today, you will discover that she was not, as we mistakenly tend to remember her, the first man to undergo transsexual surgery; she was the first man to have made a big splash in the papers for doing it — an American GI who went to Denmark to get his sex changed, generating such headlines as, "GI GOES ABROAD AND COMES BACK A BROAD," but that's not how I remember her. What has stuck in my head is not her personal story but the details of how they did it to her — the hormones, the surgery. When I first heard about her, I knew instantly — knew at a deep visceral level — exactly why a boy would want to do that. I also knew that I didn't want to do that.

What I learned from Christine's story was that there was a way for medical science to make men into women — but what did that mean for me? Now that I knew for sure that I was a boy, there were times when I wanted to be a girl — or thought that I should have been a girl — but I didn't want to have surgery and lose the parts I'd been born with. It wasn't that I loved those parts — I felt a certain ambivalence toward them, actually — it had to do with wanting to maintain the integrity of my body, and the thought of getting those parts cut off filled me with horror. We now know that transgender girls often feel trapped in the wrong body. That was never true of me. I felt trapped in *something*, but I knew that an operation wouldn't get me out of it.

If I'd been a few years older, I might have thought what most grown-ups in the 1950s must have thought — that Christine Jorgensen had done it because she'd wanted to have sex with men — but that's very much an adult idea, and it never entered my mind. I knew from reading about the ancient Greeks that boys sometimes had boyfriends and girls sometimes had girlfriends, but, like many other strange and interesting things, that must happen *somewhere else*, because it clearly didn't happen in the Wheeling, West Virginia, that I knew. As a science fiction reader, I was used to seeing things from a galactic point of view, so I didn't find the notion of people having sex with others of their own sex either shocking or even particularly surprising. It felt as normal to me as anything else. I hadn't been hit by even the first early distant warnings of puberty yet, so sex for me was purely theoretical — a story about grown-ups — and the most I could imagine for myself was a kiss. But if anybody had told me that Christine Jorgensen's desire to be transformed into a woman had anything to do with sex, I would not have understood it. How could it have anything to do with sex? If you were a boy who wanted to be turned into a girl, it obviously had to do with *who you wanted to be.*

## 2

KATHY, the girl I might have been, had not gone away, and she never would, but she'd retreated into another dimension like a science fiction creature living in a parallel universe. In her honor, I read *Seventeen Magazine*, painted my fingernails, and wandered through department stores looking for clothes she would have liked had I been able to wear them. Then there was the other boy I might have been, the one who'd been named after his father. I imagined Eugene Charles Maillard the Fourth wearing shorts and a beret, speaking French, and living in Canada with other Maillards who had brown eyes and spoke French. In his honor, I bought myself a beret and tried to learn French from Linguaphone records. But Keith Maillard? I didn't know about him.

My mother had said that I deserved my own name so she'd named me after Keith Alexander in *Tap Roots* by James Street. That big fat book had always been there, waiting for me to get around to it. Who was Keith Alexander? That's what everybody else wanted to know too.

The "stranger in town" is a stock figure in American popular writing, but that was the first I'd seen of him, and I read the story of Keith Alexander's arrival as though it was brand new. He rides into town on a white stallion with a silver-tipped saddle and sets all tongues to wagging. From the way he sits on a horse, some say he must be from Kentucky. No, others say, with his English saddle and jet-black hair, he must be Irish — Black Irish. But he's a fop. Look at those fancy clothes — he must be French. He walks like a soldier from West Point, says "about" like a Virginian, but he blurs his vowels like a fool from Tennessee —

Keith Alexander is a cold, bitter man who never laughs. His dueling pistols are called Alpha and Omega. He keeps them in a silk-lined case. With Alpha in his left hand, he can snuff a candle at forty paces; with Omega in his right, he can trim a man's beard at fifty. Seventeen men have asked him, "Who are you and where are you from?" and he has answered them all at dawn under the oaks behind the state capital.

MY OFFICIAL PUBLIC POSITION has always been that reading is good for you — that everybody, even kids, should be allowed to read anything they want — but privately, I'm not so sure. Only twice have I encountered something I knew I shouldn't be reading, something that would hurt me if I kept on going. One was a poisonous little story by Pierre Louÿs, the other one of H.P. Lovecraft's weird tales that was soaked even more than usual in the author's hopelessly alienated sensibility. In both cases I hit a block of resistance inside myself that said, "You shouldn't be reading this . . .

not right now," and had enough sense to put the book down. Nothing told me that I shouldn't be reading *Tap Roots.*

In my memory it's a huge door-stopper of a book, as big as the Bible, but returning to it now, I see that it's a modest 593 pages, something that an avid reader like myself at eleven could have sailed through in a week of late nights. It's not a great novel by any means, but it's a page-turner that cracks right along, tells the story of a family in an anti-slavery section of Mississippi that didn't want to go with the Confederacy, that seceded from the secession. "What does 'tap roots' mean?" I'd asked my mother when I was little, and she'd told me that they were tree roots that went down deep into the earth — the way that the Dabneys in the book had tap roots sunk deep into the soil of Mississippi. I got that right away because I had always been told that we had tap roots sunk deep into the soil on both sides of the Ohio River.

The book is the second of family sagas that followed the Dabneys, but the main character is Keith Alexander. He dominates the story from the moment he appears. He's the editor of *The Mississippi Whig*, ends all of his articles with quotations in Latin and Greek, writes flowery poetry he knows isn't much good, and he always tells the truth. I knew by then what happens to people who tell the truth, so I wasn't surprised when a mob burns down his newspaper office.

Keith Alexander is something more than a sharp dresser — he's "elegance itself." He wears only silk next to his skin, Irish lace on his white linen shirts, and fashionable long coats made of black broadcloth. He sleeps with silk wrapped around his lip to keep his mustache curled properly, has his long black hair shampooed with imported oils and French perfume. His dark blue eyes are nearly black — they always appear to be half shut — and his lashes are long and curved. The body inside the silk and lace is hard; he's thirty-seven and looks far younger. Women find him irresistible. Men call him "the Black Knight of Vengeance." Indians call him "the lonely one who walks with death." Near the end of the book, Keith muses that "killing is the one thing that men do well," and it's certainly something that *he* does well. To attempt to count the men that Keith Alexander kills in the pages of *Tap Roots* is a pointless exercise — they die in droves. Like Achilles, Keith might as well have been dipped in the River Styx. Nothing touches him. He's wounded once, lightly, and his only concern is the blood on his white linen shirt.

Keith Alexander is a man with no name, a bastard. His mother was the daughter of an aristocratic Kentucky bluegrass family who killed herself rather than face the disgrace of bearing a child out of wedlock. His father is a high-born Virginian. Keith hates him and says so repeatedly. He will kill anyone who dares to speak his father's name. Keith smiles out of one side of his mouth. It's a bitter, twisted, sardonic smile. Whenever he kills a man, he smiles his twisted smile.

Reading *Tap Roots* was like discovering a huge chunk of my personal puzzle that had always been missing. It excited and exhilarated me — and filled me with a bleak, dark, flat, squashed feeling. It was a weight on me to be that man, that crazy killer with his bad poetry and twisted smile, with his silk and lace and dueling pistols — that man who walked with death and was always lonely. What was my mother thinking? I don't want to believe that my mother, if she'd been fully aware of what she was doing, would have named me after a man who is driven by a passionate hatred of his father, who kills anyone who dares to inquire about his name or his origins, who says, as Keith Alexander does, "I will make my father curse the day that I was born." I don't want to believe that she would have done something like that *deliberately* — but however she did it, that's what she did.

### 3

FROM THE MOMENT I read it, Keith Alexander's thought became mine — "All lonely men understand the language of the night and the rain." I loved rain at night. I loved thunderstorms. At the first flash of lightning, I headed straight for the river. If my grandmother yelled at me to stay in the house, I didn't pay the least bit of attention. Nothing made me feel better than standing on the river bank, listening to the thunder — that big, deep hillbilly voice rolling through the hills, echoing, talking to itself — and the more lightning came forking down, the closer it got to me, the better I liked it. Damn, a thunderstorm was great; it made me laugh out loud. Like Keith Alexander, I had a charmed life. Death was my friend and constant companion, and no bolt of lightning would ever dare to strike *me*.

I don't have all the head shots taken of me each spring when the photographer came to our school, but if I did — if I lined them up in chronological order — anyone could see that something suddenly happened to my face. By the fifth grade my earlier smile is gone, replaced by what looks like a grimace or a facial tic. As I aged into my teens, I would continue to present that distorted face to any camera that was aimed at me. Bruce Dabney, the teenage boy in *Tap Roots*, practices Keith Alexander's bitter, twisted smile in the mirror. That's where I got the idea. As soon as I read about it, I put the book down, walked into the bathroom, and tried it myself.

I had Keith Alexander's name, and I was learning to wear his smile, so I was sure that there must be other things of his I could use too. I wanted a pair of toy dueling pistols I saw in a store in town, but, like many things, they were too expensive for my mother. I told my cousin Billy about the dueling pistols, and he told my uncle Bill, and within the week, Billy owned the dueling pistols. As solitary as I was — as sad as Billy was after his mom's death — there were times when each of us might have been the only friend the other had. He gave me one of the toy pistols; he'd keep the other, he said, because we were *best* friends. I wanted both, but I took what I could get. Using our backyard as the lawn behind the Mississippi state capitol in Jackson, I killed men at dawn. I practiced firing the pistol with both my left and right hand. I drew pictures of dead men lying in the mud and the rain with the tops of their heads blown off.

I kept having a nasty, horrible feeling. It was unendurable — made my entire body quiver, filled my head with dark thoughts of dying and killing, drove me out of the house in the twilight, set me to walking fast, aimlessly, around the Island or to riding my bike, furiously going nowhere. What I'm about to say is neither a metaphor nor a poetic exaggeration — I mean it literally. I would not know the proper name for that horrible feeling until it was pointed out to me in my late twenties in a therapy workshop. It was anger.

ONE AFTERNOON I was playing with some boys on a bank overlooking North Front Street. Someone had left a partially full can of house paint lying around, and one of us had pried off the lid to see what the color was — a nondescript gray. We'd left the can of paint sitting, open, at our feet in front of us. A car came driving up Front Street. Without thinking about it or planning it — without having even the faintest warning in my mind that I was going to do it — I kicked the can of paint into the path of the oncoming car.

I couldn't believe it. I'd done something terrible, something unforgivable, and I couldn't call it back.

I felt that same sense of sickening inevitability I'd felt so often before. I watched the can shooting straight for the car, a dollop of paint flinging itself free, watched the car swerve away. By some miracle, none of the paint got on the car. Thank God, I thought. The driver pulled over. Yelling, he ran straight for us.

The other boys ran away but I didn't. I deserved anything he was going to do to me. He could slap me, punch me, knock me to the ground and stomp on me. He was going to do whatever he wanted, and there was nothing I could do about it. "You goddamn little brat," he was yelling at me, "what the hell do you think you're doing?" I didn't look at him. I didn't say a word.

He towered over me, screaming. He wanted to know who my parents were. He was going to tell my parents. I didn't say a word. After a long time, he went away, and I went home. It was one of the most frightening things that had ever happened to me. I'd always suspected that I couldn't trust myself, and now I knew it. I could do something that I hadn't decided to do. I could do something that hadn't even entered my mind. I could do it in a flash, and once I'd done it, I wouldn't be able to take it back.

I ALWAYS HAD a story on the go — a complicated tale I was telling myself — and I wrote many of them down in comic-book form. The year before, in the fourth grade, I'd been working on one called *Lon of Scotland*. When he'd been a little boy, Lon, the hero of my tale, had been forced to watch while his entire family had been grue-somely slaughtered by a rival clan. He grows up, trains himself to be a great warrior, tracks down the murderers one by one, and kills them in the most ingenious ways I could devise. I'd been drawing a picture of a chopped-up man, his arms and legs scattered about on the ground in pools of blood, his face stretched into a rictus of agony, when my teacher caught me. "Don't draw pictures like that in school," she told me. OK, I thought, I'll draw them at home.

In my mind, my drawings weren't meant to be pic-tures of real men being hacked up and dismembered. I'd always known the difference between "a story" and "for real," and my drawings weren't supposed to be any more real than what I saw in *Batman* or *Superman*, but now I was deep in *Tap Roots*, and Street is a post-Hemingway writer who can describe the knife going into a man's chest so vividly that the reader becomes the one who's thrusting it and feels it when the blade strikes bone. Increasingly, the line between story and real was getting blurred for me — in matters of violence as in everything else.

**4**

I WAS HAVING SPELLS AGAIN, but I no longer called them that. I didn't call them anything. Now it wasn't just in school when I got them; sometimes they jumped me when I was alone in my room at night. I'd be lying on my bed reading, and I'd find that I couldn't concentrate, that I'd just read the same paragraph over and over and couldn't remember a word of it. I'd think, *oh no, not again,* look up to find that my vision was blurring. Then it would start — the nasty sensation on the back of my neck, the heat, the dryness in the mouth, the bass-drum heartbeat, the ghastly mental buzzing, the whole world going out of focus, turning yellow.

I learned that sitting still and trying to solve things in my mind was fatal. I had to get up and *move.* If I could pry myself off the bed, if I could walk or ride my bike, the visitation would eventually go away, but if I was in school, I was stuck with it just the way I had been at seven — *two times nine is eighteen, three times nine is twenty-seven, four times nine is thirty-six . . .*

The worst times were when I was crossing the Suspension Bridge, but then I could blame it on my fear of heights. I lived on an island, so, in order to get to town, I had to walk across that bridge. It got so bad I had to force myself to do it. Years later, when I was working at Interstate Trucking for the summer, I would confess my fear of heights to Virge, one of the mechanics, and he would warn me to stay away from heights. Virge was a man in his fifties who spoke an old-time Appalachian dialect, and what I remember him saying looks impossibly archaic when I write it down, but when I change it to more conventional English, it isn't really what he said. This is what he said: "If you're afeared of height, the height will draw ye."

It's true. Height was then, and still is for me, a conscious entity—a sucking malevolence that wants to draw me into it.

If I was walking across the bridge with other people—my mother or my cousins—I had to fight down terrible visions of pushing them over the railing. I knew that they wouldn't want to go, that they would struggle and fight back. Like a cat, they'd claw desperately, grabbing at anything. I imagined pounding the backs of their hands. I imagined prying their fingers loose, pulling them back until they snapped. I imagined their cries of anguish—heartbroken and betrayed—as they plummeted into the river.

If I was alone, it was even worse because I knew that I could do it in a flash. It would be just like when I'd kicked the paint can—I'd have no warning. It would be over so quick I couldn't do a thing about it. I'd slap both hands on the railing, hoist myself up and over. I knew I was strong enough. All it would take was a single moment, a fraction of a second, when the height said, "Now," and that would be the end of me.

Alone or in company, the only way I could make it across the bridge was to keep my eyes glued to the railing and count the bolts that held it down—*one, two, three, four, five* . . .

I started having physical symptoms—terrible pains in my stomach. I lay, doubled up in bed in a fetal position, clutching myself. Sometimes I had fierce bouts of diarrhea. My grandmother knew exactly what was wrong with me because she suffered from the same ailment. It was obviously "the Thomas Stomach" — nothing to worry about, many of her people had it in the old days. She gave me a hot water bottle to press against my cramping guts, told me to take it easy, and fed me milk toast. She knew better than to offer me what she ate for her own attacks of the Thomas Stomach — stewed tomatoes liberally sprinkled with salt, pepper, and sugar.

## 5

NEAR THE END of my fifth-grade year, Mr. Springer, the principal at Madison, called my mother in for a talk. She came back in a fury. She was mad at Zack Springer and Miss Brokaw, but she was mad at me too. It was that fifth-grade book list I'd made a point of honor not to read. Well, those books were on the West Virginia Fifth Grade Curriculum, and if I didn't read them, I couldn't get out of the Fifth Grade. "Lord, Keith, there's only a few weeks left, *and that old witch says she's not going to pass you.*"

Oh, I thought, *that's* the weird punishment — the one I'd been waiting for and dreading all year. It was simple, it was perfect, it was just about the most horrible thing I could imagine — to have to do the fifth grade *all over again with Miss Brokaw.* As punishments went, that one really took the cake. I had to hand it to Miss Brokaw. She was just as evil as I'd thought she was.

"There's nothing we can do about it," Springer had told my mother. "It doesn't matter how smart he is or how well he's doing in the rest of his schoolwork. It's required by the State Board of Education." Nobody had bothered to tell me that before.

I could see that my mother wasn't just mad, she was scared, but I wasn't. I was filled with demonic glee. I couldn't have been any happier if I'd been Keith Alexander challenged to a duel by some fumble-fingered farm boy. Those idiots at Madison had thought they'd got me, but they had another think coming. They'd been so stupid that they'd attacked me in the one area where I was better than they were, and now I had a chance to beat them at their own game. In less than a week I read what was required — five of the books on the West Virginia Fifth Grade Curriculum — and wrote reports on them. They were good reports too. Evil as she was, Miss Brokaw must have had a streak of good old-fashioned justice in her because she gave me As on them.

So I passed the fifth grade, and I thought *to hell with all of you* and went off to day camp the way I always did every summer. I forgot about the whole thing, but my mother didn't.

SURELY ANY ADULT who had bothered to take a good look at me would have noticed that something was going

124

wrong, but if anybody did notice, nobody was doing anything about it. West Virginia is a mind-your-own-business place that tolerates considerable eccentricity — at least in those folks whose people have been there for a long time — and down at my kid level, it never occurred to me that anybody was paying any attention to me whatsoever. I was left alone in my splendid and scary isolation.

When I was at day camp, I did my best to act like a real boy, but when I was at home, I went off in another direction. I vaguely remember — I *think* I can remember — that I wanted to see how long I could let my hair grow that summer. What I do remember is spending hours looking at myself in the mirror, practicing Keith Alexander's bitter twisted smile, combing my hair one way and then another.

My problem was not that I had no idea of what was going on. My problem was that I had *far too many ideas* — but none that I could count on to remain true for very long. In those moments when I could rise above my inner debates to see myself debating, what terrified me was my inability to find anything stable. There were always too many possibilities — so many they seemed infinite. My mental state was something like a grid made up of nodes that continually zapped current back and forth. Each node had a toggle switch so that the energy could be made to flow either way — that is, anything that I thought could instantly turn into its opposite — and any term in the grid could be replaced by another term.

Here's a short version of it.

My real name is [is not] Keith [Eugene, Kathy].
I am [am not] like Keith Alexander.
I am [am not] like my father.
I am [am not] a boy [a girl].
I do [don't] like pretending to be a girl [boy].
I am [am not] like Christine Jorgensen.
I do [don't] want to grow up.
When I grow up I will [will not] be a man.

I COULDN'T SHAKE myself free of Keith Alexander. I had his name, didn't I? I took *Tap Roots* and everything in it to be "true" — that is, I thought that it was exactly like some of the books they gave us in school, history written as a novel, except bigger and intended for adults — but however much it masquerades as realism, *Tap Roots* is a thriller, and a thriller is required to end in violence. "There was a new feeling, an exhilaration, about Keith Alexander, and the birth of the day gave birth to an exuberance within him. He was going to fight." Keith kills his dastardly rival, Clay — sneaks through the Confederate lines and blows him away before anyone can stop him — and then escapes back to his own lines to lead his men into the climactic battle that will leave most of them dead.

Try as we will to be anywhere else, we're stamped with our own time as firmly as a coin is stamped in a mint. *Tap Roots* tells us as much about the early '40s when it was written as it does about the Civil War era when it is set. It's no accident that the book was published as the United States was entering the last war that the vast majority of Americans would feel good about fighting. Keith forgets his true love, forgets everything except his pistols and his enemies. He muses that "love is the thing women live and men share, but war is a man's work."

When Bruce, the youngest Dabney, kills his first man, Keith, with his bitter smile, says, "That's it. That's all there is to it."

A "crushing load" lifts from Bruce's heart, and he giggles. He thinks how easy it is to kill. It's like shooting rabbits. He starts to sing, continues to aim and fire, loses himself in the excitement. As Street tells it through the filter of Keith Alexander's consciousness — in that lost moment of excitement, Bruce "crossed that mysterious gulf between boyhood and manhood, and when he came into manhood he had a gun in his hand and was doing the one thing that men do well, killing other men . . ."

"Don't think about who they are," Keith Alexander tells him. "Just shoot them."

MY MOTHER HAD named me Keith because I deserved my own name, but I didn't have my own name, I had Keith Alexander's name. Someone else looking at me would have seen a strange little boy playing alone, but I wasn't alone. The empty space around me was crowded with James Street's characters, brought to life by his words —

Keith brought Alpha to position, aimed at the yellow sash, and fired.

Clay jerked upright and he lowered his own pistol, but calmly, surely, Keith aimed Omega between the man's eyes, and the powerful charge, a large ball and two small ones, blew open his forehead and he pitched headlong from his horse and fell on his right shoulder and his body slid in the mud and his blood and brains ran into the ooze.

I imagined myself into James Street's book. Do you want to know why I shot him first through the yellow sash? To shoot him through the guts, that's why. That's the most horrible way to kill a man. I'd wanted him to feel excruciating pain, wanted him to have a second or two to understand what was happening, to know that he'd lost and I'd won, to know that he was going to die. Then, with the shot between the eyes, I'd put him out of his misery. Death was my friend and walked at my side. Seventeen men had asked me, "Who is your father?" and I'd answered every one of them with a powerful charge, a large ball and two small ones, fired straight through their mouths.

Sometimes I didn't bother to put them out of their misery but let them lie in the mud and the rain, clutching their guts, suffering the worst pain imaginable, as they took hours, even days, to die their slow, excruciating deaths — and I drew them like that, their eyes stretched wide, their screaming mouths pried open, their guts spilled out in ropey loops. Smiling my bitter, twisted smile, I lay on my desk in the thickening evening and shot at pigeons on our neighbor's garage roof. The air gun was my cousin Billy's, a pump rifle, and it was nowhere near powerful enough to do the job.

I could see the BBs in the air — their slow curving trajectory. My first shots fell far below my target; the pigeons burst into flight. Each time I waited patiently for them to land, to settle down, so I could try again. They were so stupid they kept coming back just as though nothing was happening. I was compensating, raising my aim, getting closer, and I might have got one, but our neighbor called on the phone to my grandmother, and she yelled at me to stop.

I was bitterly disappointed. I knew that I'd have to get a real rifle someday, one that shot real bullets. I knew that in order to become a man, I would have to kill. Once I'd killed, I'd feel no remorse. No-name bastards feel no remorse.

## 6

ONE AFTERNOON, bored, I followed the step-by-step instructions I'd found in one of my mother's magazines and gave myself an obsessively thorough manicure. I soaked my hands, pushed down my cuticles, shaped my nails, and painted them — one layer of base coat, three of polish, and one of top coat. The way you did a

French finish in those days was by coloring the undersides of your nails with a white pencil, but those white lines vanished the minute you washed your hands, so I painted the undersides of my nails with white oil paint. When my mother saw me, she said, "Get that damn nail polish off yourself."

I was shocked and hurt. I'd been wearing clear nail polish off and on for years. Other boys had teased me sometimes, but I'd never got into any serious trouble, and I'd never before heard a word from my mother about it. "I want to talk to you," she said.

Conversations that she considered "personal" were not my mother's strong suit; they garbled her tongue, focused her eyes onto some imaginary spot in the airy distance, and screwed her face into a death mask. Her embarrassment was infectious; within minutes I would become just as awkward as she was. By unspoken mutual consent that lasted until she died at nearly ninety-four, we attempted as few personal conversations as possible. The one we had that night was one of the worst. She didn't simply tell me what was on her mind; she opened with a long preamble about herself — how hard it was trying to be "both a mother and a father to you."

Now I have considerable sympathy for her. I must have been driving her up the wall. When I'd been little, she'd allowed me to paint myself with rouge and lipstick and had never made me feel ashamed about it. Guessing that I might be like my father, she'd offered me tap lessons. She would have let me wear girls' tap shoes if I'd wanted to, but she'd drawn the line at putting me into a girl's class — that would have been too much. When I'd discovered my Scots heritage, she'd taken me to visit my girl cousins, but she must have had a long chat with their mom so that when I showed up in my kilt, it wouldn't be a big deal. She'd never said a word about the ballet girls I'd taped up all over my walls, and she'd never commented on any of the odd outfits I sometimes wore, but she must have been thinking exactly what anybody else in the '50s would have mistakenly been thinking — boys who are like girls can grow up to be men who are like women, and men who are like women are homosexuals, but if you saw it coming, you could nip it in the bud.

At eleven I was too deeply stuck in my own predicament to have any sympathy for her; I just wanted this horrible conversation to be over. After about the eighth or tenth long deadly silence, she managed to say, "You're too much like a girl. You've got to stop this." It wasn't just the nail polish. That was okay sometimes. But *I was just going too far with it.*

I suspected that she might be right — or at least right enough — but I was appalled at where she was seemed to be going. If she crossed a certain line, my only defense would be to say nothing, admit to nothing, and just wait her out. "It's my own fault," she said. "There's no men in your life. I'm sorry. But you have to stop this."

Sometimes I stood like a girl, she said. That was news to me. What on earth could it possibly mean — standing with your feet together? Or standing with them apart?

I didn't have a clue. There were other things too. I talked like a girl, she said. That one hurt me to the quick. If someone had asked me to talk like a girl, I wouldn't have known how to begin. I'd stopped playing with girls a long time ago, and now I didn't know any girls well enough to talk *to* them, let alone talk *like* them. I knew I used big fancy words — things I read in books. Is that what she meant? Or something else? I felt a hopeless despair.

"Would you like to go to Linsly?" she said.

Linsly? That was an all-boys military school. Linsly cadets wore uniforms and marched around with guns. "I've had it with Madison," she said. "I'm sick of those dictatorial old maid school teachers like Sarah Brokaw. They don't like you. They're never going to like you. You're not learning anything there. You'd get a darned good education at Linsly."

I didn't care about a darned good education. I knew that wherever I went to school, I'd do just as well as I always had, but I liked the thought of wearing a uniform and learning to shoot a gun. If I wanted to be more like Keith Alexander, that would be the place to do it.

MY MOTHER HAD BEEN brooding about me for a while. She'd had a long chat with the nice man who sold us insurance. He'd gone to Linsly, had been a great football player there, and he told her to send me to Linsly. "Lord," my mother had said, "we don't have that kind of money."

"Well, he's bright, isn't he? Maybe they'll give him a scholarship."

The headmaster was a tall, imposing man with a distinguished thatch of silver hair — and I know the words I've just used to describe him are clichés, but he wore them well. He had a distinctive voice — a loud, penetrating, nasal voice. Any Linsly cadet could imitate that dreaded voice in half a second, but it's damnably difficult to describe with words on a page; neither "drawl" nor "whine" are even close to right, but they get it into the ballpark. He scared the crap out of me.

My mother and I sat in the headmaster's office. I was wearing a suit and tie for the occasion, and I'd just had my hair cut. My mother told the headmaster that I was a certified, number-one whiz kid, and she had my school transcripts to prove it. Except for gym, I'd never received anything lower than an A in my life.

"How much support does he get from his father?" he asked.

Ah, the checks arriving in the mail once a month, the ones with never a word attached to them. My mother said, "Twenty-two dollars a month."

He said, "All right, if you can buy his uniforms, his tuition here is twenty-two dollars a month. You can get his uniforms used. They're not that expensive. He's got a scholarship at Linsly if he wants it."

Did I want it? They were both looking at me. "Sure," I said. I knew I was supposed to say something more — this was my big moment — so I managed a few words about how I would just love going to Linsly. "Thank you," I said.

As we were getting ready to leave, my mother said, "Oh, there's one more thing. He's grown up with no men in his life, and he's too much like a girl."

I had never been so embarrassed.

"Don't worry," the headmaster said, "we'll take care of that."

*part IV*

# THE PINK SHIRT

## 1

A SEARING ENERGY, wordless as pain, attaches itself to the year I was thirteen. 1955 was the year the Fort Henry Bridge opened and cut the Island in half, destroying forever the landscape of my childhood home — the year my hormones first began to hit me, the year I heard "Maybellene" on the radio — the year I saw *The Blackboard Jungle*, *The Cobweb*, *The Seven Year Itch*, and *Rebel Without a Cause* — the year James Dean died. If I was part of "a generation" — and I was — that was the year I joined it.

I'd been alarmingly thin as a child, but later, as I approached puberty, I'd put on enough weight to see myself as chubby. At thirteen I decided to do something about it, tried out every wacko diet that appeared in my mother's magazines, carried a calorie counter around in my pocket, added up my meals, and vowed to live on the drop-dead minimum. I pushed aside rice or potatoes, peeled the bun off hamburgers and ate only the meat. I lived for days on a concoction made of skimmed milk, raw eggs, and orange juice. Eating felt dirty to me; hunger was a victory. I did not want to grow up to be big and strong; I wanted to be as slender as a grass stem, as agile as quicksilver, and as small as possible.

I wore a pink shirt when I was thirteen. Up until then, boys could not wear pink. I did not put that strongly enough. Up until then, there had been *no possible way in hell* a boy could wear pink — but then suddenly, out of nowhere, pink was cool. The shirt was made of a crinkly nylon and was transparent — not as sheer as a pair of stockings, but sheer enough so that you could see my skin right through it. I admired myself in a full-length mirror. I loved the way my stomach made a concavity under my rib cage.

That pink shirt radiates so much symbolic force that I could swing an entire narrative around it. Other images are drawn to it, cluster around it. Rain smeared the streets and made them reflect light as I walked around the Island, aware of myself. I sensed an enormity, gleaming and inexhaustible, that I hadn't even begun to touch. The sky faded into twilight, and the reflection of the streetlights rose to meet me — those smears of gray and gold and blue I tried later to capture with oil paint, which is why these memories smell like turpentine.

Susan Strasberg was the first actress I ever saw who filled me with longing. In *The Cobweb* she was a teenager playing a teenager. She had the thin face of a child and huge brown eyes drenched in melancholy. I'm pretty sure that now I'd see that movie as a real turkey, but it cracked my mind open — sent me off to read the book, still looking for the girl in the movie, still pursuing the gravity of what I'd felt for her. From reading mysteries, I'd learned to see the world as a mystery, my life as a mystery, but reading *The Cobweb* took me one layer deeper. It was my first introduction to Freud — a story about an insane asylum where the people who care for the inmates are just as crazy as the inmates themselves. It was the first time I'd realized that you could see *your own mind* as a mystery.

Stories, whether in books or movies, were always part of a bigger whole — the world I was trying to construct. *Rebel Without a Cause* was far and away the most important story the year I was thirteen. For anyone of my generation, it was so good — gathered up so many power lines and wove them into such a highly charged knot — that, if you didn't know better, you might think that the people who made it actually knew what they were doing. The characters in the bizarre, perfect love triangle that forms the emotional core meet in the police station — three fucked-up teenagers played by James Dean, Natalie Wood, and Sal Mineo. We first see Jimmy lying dead drunk in the street, trying to put a child's toy to sleep. The cops grab him. Then we meet Judy, Natalie Wood's character, who's been picked up for roaming the streets at one in the morning. She tells a sympathetic cop, "He called me a dirty tramp . . . *my own father!*" Natalie's giving us a good performance. She's crying real tears.

Jimmy's been nothing but a goof so far, drunk and silly, and he goes on being nothing but a goof even after his parents show up. Then, in a second or two — with a flash in his eyes and only one line of dialogue — he blows the story right off the screen. "Do you think I'm funny?" he says to his father, and the whole universe isn't big enough to contain that flicker of rage. W H O A, I was slammed back into my seat, destroyed. I'd been going to movies since I was four, but I'd never seen anything like that.

The scene from *Rebel* I remember as absolutely central is the confrontation between Jimmy and his parents. Jimmy's mother is being played by a good old Hollywood warhorse, Ann Doran. His father is being played by Jim Backus, best known at the time as the voice of the nearsighted cartoon character "Mr. Magoo." When the scene opens, the actors are taking it moderato, reading it quietly enough to be plausible — but as soon as Jimmy tells his parents about the chicken run and the boy who died in it, Doran accelerates her performance from zero to sixty in half a second, jacks it up to full crank, and rips through her emotional beats with no holds barred. Backus, another old pro, goes right with her. Oh, my God, they're yelling, gesturing, emoting, acting the living dogfuck out of that scene. Jimmy doesn't go with them. He's reacting to them, certainly. He is, indeed, moving through the same timeline that they are, but he's in another dimension. The effect is weirdly unsettling.

Fifty years later, *Rebel* can be read as an object lesson in why a director should not try to mix two radically different acting styles. To me at thirteen, it was an object lesson in why teenagers and adults could never possibly communicate with each other. The wildly yelling, gesticulating, utterly predictable grown-ups would never get the point, not if they tried for a million years. They were acting in a movie. Jimmy, who was *one of us*, was not acting in anything. He was real.

These images hammer me, hammer me. Jimmy begging his father for help — "Dad, you've got to give me something. You've got to give me something fast." Jimmy trying to make his father see the point — "Dad? I said it was a matter of honor? Remember? They called me chicken. You know? Chicken? I had to go. Because if I didn't, I'd never be able to face those kids again." Jimmy finally getting all of his anguish boiled down into one line — *"Dad, stand up for me."*

Sal Mineo plays a brainy slender kid, nicknamed "Plato," who was enough like me that I felt the sharp click of identification and then denied it immediately. The family maid has come to the police station to bring him home. He's been arrested for shooting puppies. I'd never killed anything, but I understood his grief and bleak satisfaction. I knew why he'd killed the puppies. "Where's his father?" the cop asks.

"Oh," the maid says, "we haven't seen him in a long time."

Now, watching the opening of *Rebel*, I can retrieve the wordless density in myself, and the rain, walking by the river, and the tangle — important, dark, just beyond the edge of comprehension. I wanted to grow up to be like Jimmy in exactly the same way that when he was on the screen, he blotted everyone else out. He embodied everything that couldn't be solved. He was brave, brash, tender, vulnerable, fucked-up, tough, barely articulate, and beautiful. I wanted to be as beautiful as he was. I walked the streets of Wheeling at night, alert and distant, and read everything as a clue.

## 2

"GET OUT OF THE VALLEY" — that was. my mother's mantra. She began telling me that when I was scarcely old enough to understand the literal meaning of the words and kept on repeating it until, in my early twenties, I did leave. "The Ohio Valley" was a metaphor. What I was supposed to leave behind was genteel poverty — the bleak, banal, unrelenting, soul-destroying daily grind of the working poor. The way out was through *education*. I was supposed to get a good basic education at Linsly, and I did. But the first year was hard on me. I remember an incident from a science class. When our teacher asked if any of us knew the common name for cirrus clouds, I said, "Mare's tails."

One of my classmates said — in an awed, spontaneous outburst — "Isn't there *anything* you don't know?"

I was flattered at first, but then, after I thought about it a moment, it felt creepy. Of course I'd had some experience with boys, but now I was in an all-boys world, and I knew that being smart would only take me so far. Boys had a rough, hard edge to them that scared and intimidated me; their teasing could be unremitting and merciless. I was already getting called "Einstein."

One morning somebody did something to me. I don't remember what, but it was the kind of thing that happened all the time — I got the books knocked out of my hands or was shoved into a locker. I started to cry and couldn't stop. I wasn't sobbing. It was just a steady trickle of tears down my cheeks. I remember thinking, *this is just too hard*.

At first I got shit for it, but eventually the other boys began to worry about me, asking, "What's the matter? Are you all right?" I couldn't say anything. In class, so my teachers wouldn't notice, I pretended that my nose was running, sat with my handkerchief pressed against my face. I cried all through lunch period. By afternoon my classmates were involved in a conspiracy to cover up for me. "He's okay," they said to our teachers. "He's just got a cold."

I wasn't stuck in the dorm. I was a day student, and I kept thinking, I've got to stop acting like a girl or I'll never be able to come back here. I'd been crying all day, and I still couldn't stop. My classmates kept giving me — and each other — looks of gloomy concern. This was my first experience of the kind of male bonding that was foundational to the culture of our school. An unwritten code dictated that boys had to protect each other — they even had to protect a new kid who wasn't dry behind the ears yet — and when it came down to the crunch, it was *us, the boys,* against *them, the officers and teachers.*

Near the end of the day, another boy — I remember nothing about him except that he was a lot bigger than I was — drew me off to one side, took hold of my shoulders and squeezed them. I stood there with tears leaking down my face. "Keith," he said in a clear, firm, emphatic voice, *"everything is going to be all right."* I believed him and stopped crying. It would be years before anyone would see me cry again. As time passed, I learned that you do not cry, ever, under any circumstances — and if possible, you do not show *any* emotion. During my seven years in military school, I acquired the ability to put on a face that gave away nothing.

In the spring of our graduating year one of our classmates came to school early, dead drunk, and fired his rifle into the lockers lining the walls of the hall where we were taught riflery. The code had been absolutely ground into our bones by then, and this was not a matter that we had to discuss — there was absolutely no way those in authority should ever know that this had happened, and none of them ever did. All of us admired the bullet hole in the lockers.

3

WHEN I WAS ELEVEN, my cousins came to live with us. I can't remember exactly what my mother told me about it — something about Uncle Bill having to work out of town — but I didn't really care and didn't pay much attention. Rather than feeling put upon, I thought it was going to be fun, and it was. Like the characters in the Shakespeare plays we read in school, we called each other "cos." I liked having a girl in the house — watched with fascination as Becky added layer upon layer of petticoats and crinolines to give her skirt the enormous poof required by the style of the time, and Billy had always been in my life, that familiar kid a year younger — my dependable sidekick, my almost brother. He and I shared a room in the attic. It took me a while to get over my fear of the ghosts who roamed up there at night, and I slept with a Bible next to my bed to ward them off.

It wasn't until my grandmother was in her nineties and lost her inner censor that I heard this story. She'd gone down to visit Bill in his apartment on the south end of the Island. He had run the W.C. Brown Company into bankruptcy by then and was working as a night clerk in a hotel. When she walked in, she found her son drunk as a lord and Billy and Becky crying their eyes out. "What on *earth* is going on?" she asked them.

Billy was crying too hard to talk, but Becky said, "Dad's going to put us in a Home."

"I just can't do it anymore," Bill said. "I can't support them. My wife's dead. I can't do it. I've got to put them in the Children's Home."

My grandmother always knew what was right. "You're going to do nothing of the kind. They're coming home with me."

BILLY HAD ALWAYS been a difficult child. He was quiet, even shy, but there had always been something dangerous about him — the sleepwalking, the legendary dozen eggs, the fires. The adults kept asking each other, "What are we going to do with Billy?" He had problems in school, and his teachers mistakenly took him for dull, so they eventually put him into the industrial arts program at Wheeling High — not necessarily a good idea, I thought, when I came home one afternoon and found him sitting on the edge of his bed with an arc welder fired up and raining eye-blistering sparks onto the carpet.

For several months Billy spent much of his spare time trying to make gunpowder. Why he wanted to do that was, to him, fairly obvious — if he had gunpowder, he could *blow things up*. I don't know where he bought the ingredients, but he had big boxes of sulfur, charcoal, and potassium nitrate. The encyclopedia told him the right proportions, but no matter what he did, his mixtures never exploded, they only burned. One hot summer's afternoon when there was nobody at home but us, he tried out his ultimate bomb test. He'd stuffed a length of cardboard tubing with his gunpowder mix and sealed it with paraffin. He knew how to make fuses by then, and they worked just fine. He put his bomb — it looked like a miniature stick of dynamite — on the back-porch railing, lit it, and we ran to the far end of the yard and waited for what we hoped would be an explosion. Instead it made a dull low throaty T H U M P and sent up a thick roiling plume of black smoke. It had *sort of* exploded, we decided — well, no, it hadn't *really* exploded — but whatever it had done, it had left behind a fairly substantial hole in the railing, and we felt like two prime idiots. We sanded down the hole and repainted it, leaving a huge dent, shiny with new paint. If anyone ever noticed, we never heard about it.

On another occasion, Billy decided to try out an old longbow we'd found in the attic — a fairly formidable hunk of wood that took all of his strength to draw. He stood at the far side of our bedroom and shot arrows through the open door to the storage area where they were supposed to land in a cardboard box he'd set up as a target. When he missed, as he occasionally did, the arrows stuck in the wall. I came bounding up the stairs, and he missed my head — honest to God, this is true — by a matter of inches. After any of his disasters, he was always sorry. There was something large, bumbling, and endearing about him. I can still see his hapless shrug and bemused, apologetic grin.

One Sunday afternoon Billy and I came sickeningly close to killing my mother. Among the many objects that had flowed from Billy's house to our house after his mother died was a massive bookcase. It was from the late Victorian era when furniture was supposed to be just as substantial as your life — when things were supposed to be heavy, solid, and able to sit where you put them forever, waiting for your kids to inherit them. This one was mahogany, I believe — anyhow a dark wood — and had glass doors. My bedrooms were always drowning in books, so my mother had decided to put that bookcase in the attic room I shared with Billy. She'd had some men haul it up there and plant it right in front of the banister at the top of the stairs. Of course I'd crammed every shelf.

As a little kid, I hadn't learned the kind of play fighting that boys do — we called it "horsing around"— but I learned it later, at Linsly, because I didn't have any choice in the matter. Like friendly brothers, Billy and I did a lot of horsing around — chasing each other, yelling, wrestling, laughing, trying to pin each other — and that afternoon we must have been making a lot of noise. My mother yelled at us a few times to cut it out, but we didn't pay any attention, so she started up the stairs to give us a piece of her mind. She later attributed her salvation to some form of divine intervention — "To this day I don't know what told me to turn around and go back down."

Whatever voice was warning her, she listened to it and made a mad dash back down the stairs just as Billy and I knocked the bookcase over the banister. It fell directly behind her, exploding — books and shattered wood and broken glass flying everywhere. She'd been less than two feet from where it came down; miraculously, nothing had hit her. I'm not even going to try to describe the sound it made.

Billy, my mother, and I of course had to discuss the matter. We ended up sitting at the kitchen table as she lectured us with the intensely focused adrenaline-fueled fury of someone who has just come close to being killed. Guilty as sin, Billy and I sat there silently, hoping she would eventually stop. As she was hammering us with her merciless barrage of words, Billy's hands were automatically stuffing matches into a small round match container. Both my mother and I must surely have seen what he was doing, but it must not have registered. He stuffed them in until he couldn't possibly cram in another one, then screwed the lid on tight and the whole works exploded in his hands. We stared at each other, too shocked to speak. He wasn't badly burned.

**4**

MY MOTHER HAD good reasons for becoming the only New Deal Democrat in a family of Republicans: as soon as she graduated from high school, she was never unemployed until she retired in her sixties. While my cousins were living with us, she was supporting six people — herself, my grandmother, my grandmother's aunt Deal, Becky, Billy, and me. During my last years at Linsly, she organized the office staff at the trucking company where she was working, and they joined the Teamster's Union. The company got even with her by promoting her to a management position and firing her. She immediately got another job at Bellaire Garment across the river where she managed an office full of "girls" and did the entire payroll. At one point she asked for a raise. Her boss said, "Aileen, you're already one of the highest-paid women in the Ohio Valley." That meant that she was getting paid not much more than a man in an entry-level clerical job. Her life was, to use one of her favorite words, "rough." She got through the worst of it with a little help from Household Finance. It took her years to pay them back.

"Follow the money" is a pretty good way to get to the roots of any story. My mother's first job was with Uncle Will Brown, the pioneering Ohio Valley photographer. She can tell her own story better than I can. I recorded this interview with her when she was well into her eighties, but sorrow and anger were still sounding clearly in her voice.

I graduated in '29. That was the period that I turned against Dad. Everybody was going away to school in the fall, and I had my room paid for, reserved. We'd been saving money for years. Mother and I worked on clothes all summer.

I had my wardrobe ready. I had these good-looking clothes to go to— I was going down to Athens, to Ohio University. I'd been accepted. I had my room. I'd corresponded with the girl I was going to room with. And Dad came home and says, "Well, you can't go. I lost all your money in a poker game." Says, "I was trying to get you double what I had— lost it all."

So that's that. I turned against him. I never forgave him, really. Even today, I can't— Because— *Lord, Keith, I was college material.*

I was crushed. It just knocked it out of me. Everybody— all the girls that I knew were going to college. Either up to West Liberty, or Bethany, or down to West Virginia. I didn't get to go. But— I was so crazy about Dad. In time it was just kind of a thing of the past. Mother never forgave him for building me up to the point of going to school and then coming home and saying, "You can't go." It was just one thing after the other like that, ah— and she never forgave him. That's really hard to do to a kid, you know. Especially an eighteen-year-old that had the world on a string. But— I survived it.

So after Dad lost the money and I couldn't go to school, I went to work for Uncle Will Brown at eleven dollars a week. Uncle Will was the mainstay at that point, and he told Mother, he says, "You send her over."

My mother worked for Uncle Will as long as she could stand it, and then she got a bookkeeping job at Hazel Atlas. Eventually Uncle Will retired and turned the business over to Addison, the responsible nephew.

Bill went down to the Fostoria Glass and got a good job and drank himself out of it. So he came up, and he bellyached to Mother, and Mother to Aunt Deal. "Well, you just go in the shop and work with Addison." Which was definitely the wrong thing to do. I was out at the Hazel Atlas and should have stayed there. Skipper Cobb was my boss out there, and when I told him I was quitting to go out and take care of the shop and the books for Bill and Addison, he said, "Don't do it. Do *not* do it! I beg you, don't do it." But Mother was pushing, so I went.

The two brothers hated each other and never spoke. Eventually Addison got so sick of Bill's drinking that he sold the business to him for a dollar and moved to Buffalo where he was employed by Eastman Kodak for the rest of his working life. That left my mother working for her brother Bill.

Bill was drinking like a fish, but he always had good clothes and dressed like a fashion plate. Bill wore clothes well. He was big enough to carry them. He was flitting from bar to bar.

You know what I mean? Bill would do anything—
no, I won't say *anything*— if he didn't have to
work. He made friends so— I don't know. Bill was
a sponger. He expected somebody to take care of
him. Which Mother did. All he wanted to do was
just have the best clothes— which he had. And
Mother would sit up till midnight sewing in order
to keep food on the table, and he'd take ten dollars
from her and go gamble. Bill was a— I don't— I
won't use the word "favorite," but Bill could do no
wrong in Mother's eyes. Drink. Gamble. "Oh, he's
just like his father." You know, Bill was a likable
person. And I liked him. But he would not work.

My life wasn't what it should have been,
because Dad was a gambler. He lost everything
he made. He didn't work. He just piddled around
and gambled. That's the reason Mother left him.
And Bill was very much the same type person.
Mother was working, I was working, Addison
was working, and Bill would not work. Bill
would take bread out of a person's mouth rather
than earn it— and I resented it. I went through
a period that I was bitter that I didn't have the
backing that I should have had. But— it taught
me a lot about men. It wasn't like today. Today's
girls are on an equal footing with the men in
business. They've earned it up through the years.
But back then, ah— men expected a hell of a lot
out of a girl. I'm surprised I made it.

At that point in time— I don't know whether it's changed; I don't know anything about the business world today— but a man was out to get all he could get and didn't hesitate. I don't know how I ever got through all that. Well, I wasn't the only one. Every girl that worked at that point, and had contact with men, would tell you the same thing. A man would do anything to take advantage of a female, and a girl just had to fight her way through the years for respect. And it wasn't easy. I've met a lot of nice men. I've met a lot of scoundrels.

I shouldn't have spent seven years in a blueprint shop. I worked hard that seven years. That was a hell of a job. And Bill was taking every cent that came in. You'd go in on Monday morning, and he would have written a check for everything that was in the bank. Those were my hell years.

**5**

UNAWARE OF HOW LUCKY I was, I did the only thing my mother ever asked me to do — got good grades. Schoolwork was easy for me, and I'll always be grateful for the vast amounts of leftover time I had. I learned far more from following my interests through the Ohio County Public Library than I did in any classroom.

After I read Freud's *Introduction to Psychoanalysis* in high school, I tried to see myself in a detached, nearly clinical way as though I were my own case history, so I became an archivist of my life and saved nearly every word I had written between the ages of thirteen and eighteen. I organized that material, divided grade school writing from high-school writing, dated it as best I could, and stored it in file boxes. I was well along into writing this book before I remembered those archives and hauled them out of the back of a closet. The last time I'd read some of that stuff had been shortly after I'd written it. I expected to find a few scraps of silly juvenilia, nothing terribly interesting. Instead I found hundreds of handwritten pages that revealed much of my earlier self. I did remember some of those stories, but not very well. Others I'd forgotten so completely that they might as well have been written by someone else — a clever but annoying kid I'd known long ago.

In my grade school stories there are lots of cops, private eyes, teenage hoods, bad girls in tight skirts, and tortured artists, but no one resembles anyone I actually knew. Feminine boys often appear — boys who take ballet classes, have girls for best friends, and are so pretty that they are often mistaken for girls. There's a single science fiction yarn set on a planet with a savagely turbulent wet season of continuous thunderstorms and gale-force winds — and if we want a metaphor for adolescence, that's a pretty good one. The mothers who appear are either ground-down immigrant women or shrewish stage moms who make their daughters' lives miserable. The fathers are, by and large, drunken assholes. Nearly every story has at least one dancer and somebody from France. I was attracted to exotic protagonists — like a boy-girl pair who work the two-hundred-foot sway pole in the circus. I couldn't spell worth a shit. A small fragment titled "*The Assassens*" stars "a world famous balerina," "a Russian singer and courtisan," and "the ruthless head of the French Comminist Party."

I wish that the earliest surviving example of my fiction was anything other than what it is — a first-person narrative told in a goofy, stylized, written-out dialect that I must have taken to be the cool voice of the '50s hood.

It is the first day of school and I am walking
there, when I see this reel cool chick standen' ona
bridge. Even though I already got a chick, I think
mabey I'll walk over an' pass the time of day,
which I do. She gives a queer look an' asks me if
I is new aroun here, which I is. So she says to me,
"Then you don't know who I am." An I inform
her I don't, and am waiting for her to tell me
when a tough comes over. He has a mug so ugly
it could mabey turn milk to cheese or sumpen.

What had I been reading? Damon Runyon? Pulp fiction accounts of teen gang rumbles? I don't know. I can date this story exactly because it's written onto the back pages of my corrected eighth-grade English assignments, so I would have written it when I was thirteen, early in the school year. I'd seen *The Blackboard Jungle* by then, and *Rebel Without a Cause* had hit the theaters at about the same time that I was writing this story.

My teenagers — "kats and chicks" — are armed to the teeth. They carry knives, chains, lengths of pipe, hatchets, and even guns. If they're not already supplied with weapons, they smash Coke bottles on the sides of buildings. The "reel cool chick" is the leader of a gang. "Let's see the color of his blood," she says, and Louie De Franko, my narrator, is forced to fight for his life.

Louie holds his own for a while, but just when he's about to be overwhelmed by sheer numbers, a mysterious kat named "Jukery" pulls up in a Mercedes-Benz and ominously emerges to save the day. What Louie likes best about Jukery is "de shiny .45 he has got in his hand."

Like a low-budget kung fu movie, this scrap of writing does nothing but leap from one fight sequence to the next, ramping up the violence which I've imagined in meticulous detail. When they're hurt, my characters groan, scream, bellow, and bawl. They spit out broken teeth, crawl away broken, trailing blood. When Louie has beaten one of his antagonists into submission, he levers the boy's arm up against the side of a building and kicks it, snapping the bone. After attempting for a dozen pages to fight their way to high school, Louie and Jukery finally give it up as a hopeless cause, retire to Jukery's hotel room, and get drunk.

When I read that story again at sixteen, it embarrassed the hell out of me. I saw it as utterly phony — that is, as a bunch of crap written by a girlish little boy who'd never been in a serious fight in his life. I was tempted to throw it away, but I didn't. I'd come to think of myself as a mystery to be solved, and I wanted to save the evidence.

So how do I read the evidence all these years later? Tales of teen gangs and rumbles had just begun to appear in popular culture — to alarm adults and excite teenagers — so at least part of what I was doing was gluing myself into my generation, but something else was going on too. Violence meant "male" to me, and the more graphic, painful, and revolting I could make it, the more male I would be. I had not forgotten that melancholy and terrible man, Keith Alexander, who'd given me my name, but even if I hadn't learned it from him, I would have learned it somewhere because it was deeply engrained in the culture and the message was always the same. War is a man's work, and violence is what a man does.

**6**

THE YEAR I WAS FOURTEEN I had my first wet dream. By then, I'd read everything I could on sex and sexuality, so I knew perfectly well what was happening, and my reaction took me completely by surprise. I was nauseated. It wasn't one of those "oh, gee, I think I'm going to be sick" moments; it was a violent physical force that did not allow for argument. I ran straight into the bathroom, locked the door, and threw up. I stood there sweating and alone and afraid. What I was experiencing was what we would now call "gender dysphoria." I had it big time. My mind was a thick muddy unintelligible mess. Didn't I want to be a man? If I didn't, what choice did I have? I certainly didn't want to be a woman. What did *that* mean? I felt hopelessly doomed.

By one of those unwritten rules that everyone knew, fourteen was the oldest you could be and still go trick-or-treating. I also knew that it might be the last year when I could still manage to look like a girl, so I decided to be Little Red Riding Hood. Why that particular character I don't know, although I'm guessing that I must have had some dark personal fairytale lurking just below the surface of my mind, one that involved innocence menaced by a wolf. I enlisted my cousins in this project. Billy would accompany me — he liked trick-or-treating too — and Becky would supply the clothes. The first problem was that she didn't have any red dresses, but she did have an old blue one that had the right little-kid look I wanted. Okay, I thought, I'll be Little *Blue* Riding Hood. I'd been on one wacky diet or another for over a year, and I was skinny as a toothpick, so her dress fit me fine and her shoes did too — an old pair of Mary Janes — and I added a cheap Marilyn Monroe blonde wig from the five-and-dime and a blue hood from a raincoat. I painted my fingernails fire-engine red — I'd always wanted to do that — and wore lots of red lipstick.

Something told me to do the transformation alone — that it was private — and I didn't allow anyone to see me until my costume was complete. Looking back on it, I find something significant that wasn't even faintly in my mind at the time — dressing up like a girl did not turn me on. I mean that in the most basic way. I knew by then what *did* turn me on. Kissing a girl, as I'd recently discovered — in, of all unlikely places, the choir loft of the Baptist Church — and if I wanted to turn myself on, all I had to do was remember that event. This was something else, something different.

My mother took several pictures of Billy and me, and then we stepped out into the night. We were in our own neighborhood where everybody knew everybody, so I could not possibly be anyone other than myself. I discovered immediately that the only way I could play my costume was for laughs. Lots of other kids our age were out trick-or-treating too, and their standard reaction was along the lines of, "Keith, you crazy kid, you're a riot!" I would make some sarcastic remarks about whatever costumes they were wearing and attempt to curtsy — I didn't have a clue how to curtsy — and everybody would get another good laugh, and we'd walk on until we'd run into the next group and repeat the performance. The neighbors whose doors we knocked on found me pretty funny too. "Little *Blue* Riding Hood, huh? That's a pretty deep voice you've got there, honey." All of it was good-humored enough. By the time we got home, we had plenty of candy. I took the lipstick and nail polish off myself and thought, what on earth did I do that for?

I'd been trying to connect back to that superb and magical Halloween in the third grade, but as much as playing Esmeralda had felt right, playing Little Blue Riding Hood had felt wrong. When we got the pictures back from the camera shop, I studied them for a long time. I hadn't meant to be funny, but what else could I have been? I looked about as much like a real girl as Billy, wrapped in a blanket and wearing a cheap feather head-dress, looked like a Native American. It was a damned good thing that I had been funny, because if I hadn't, how on earth could people have found any way to react to me?

The oddly perplexing thing was that I *did* know how to look like a girl — I just hadn't done it. For starters, I could have taken my glasses off, worn a bra and stuffed it with something, shaved my legs. I'd been reading Becky's *Seventeen* magazines, and they had plenty of instructions on how to put on makeup; I could have followed them. If I'd had enough money, I could have bought a real wig and a pretty dress, could have taken my time, done everything right, and then I would have looked like one of those gawky seventh-grade girls who hasn't quite got her figure yet and people who didn't know me would have thought I really was a girl. Okay, but to what purpose? To go where? To hang out with whom? *In what world?*

My demonic mental grid in which anything could instantly reverse into its opposite had become simplified by then — I wish I could say "clarified." I don't remember moving back and forth along something as clean as a spectrum — it was more like floating out into an amorphous haze and vacillating among dimly perceived landing points, nodes at which mysterious lines of force came together. Where I felt most comfortable, most myself, was at the node I'd always called "like a girl," but the ways in which I could actually be like a girl were severely limited, so I occupied that space largely in my mind. Much of the time I occupied a node where I deliberately didn't think about any of this stuff; I'd now call it "enough like a boy so there's no problem." Because I was required to do a considerable amount of acting to stay there, it also had an alien-visitor quality to it, as I watched, detached and bemused, the curious activities of these strange human beings who surrounded me. Then, at the far reaches of the amorphous haze, were two terrible nodes I tried to avoid. "Not a real boy" filled me with disgust — an unrelenting self-hatred as though I had a tumor growing around my innards and needed to burn it out. On the other side was "not a real girl," a node so painful that when I was there, I would have, if I'd had the magical ability to do it, transformed myself into a real girl in two seconds flat.

I had wanted to be Little Blue Riding Hood so I could connect my secret self to the real world, but the magic hadn't worked, and I was left feeling more alienated than before. But in the best of the Halloween pictures, I hadn't been clowning for the camera and I *had* rememberedtotakemyglassesoff. Unsmiling, nearly grave, I looked *almost* girlish with my arm draped over my cousin's shoulder, as he simply stood there — Billy, my old pal, my dependable sidekick who always went along with my schemes no matter how wacky they were.

## 7

IT SEEMS STRANGE to be writing a scene in which nothing happens, but this one persists in my autobiographical memory and replays itself at odd moments when I'm not expecting it. I am standing in my attic bedroom, looking out the window. I can't tell exactly how old I am — thirteen or fourteen — and I can't tell if it's a single event, or a number of similar events merged together, or how much I might have embellished it over the years. My sense of being alone is clear, but I can't tell if Billy is still sharing the bedroom with me and just happens not to be here at the moment or if he has already moved out. The pink shirt is hanging in an old Victorian wardrobe directly to my left. My mother paid professional movers to haul that massive piece of furniture up here. There's a full-length mirror on the front of it so I can see that I am never quite thin enough.

The bedroom is separated from the storage area by a door that's standing open. I can turn and look through that door, down an aisle between cardboard boxes and clothes racks, to the window at the far end of the attic. The light from that window and the light from the window I'm facing is the same — a rainy blue twilight. This blue, set against the tungsten yellow of light bulbs, is the provocative color of mystery.

Among the first books I bought with my own money — saving up my allowance — was a small art book of impressionist paintings; it's light like this, or the evocation of it, that thrills me, especially in the work of the late impressionists when pure representation begins to dissolve. Reflections on water, reflections of the river, reflections of streetlights on wet pavement, reflections of the signs on the hillside in Wheeling, West Virginia, reflected in the Ohio River — all of these are implied in this moment. I tried to paint it, but I never came close.

The view through the window where I am standing is not toward the street but toward the house next door. I have left a pair of black-and-white saddle shoes on the windowsill so the white polish can dry. At Linsly we stand inspection every Monday morning, so I spend at least an hour of every weekend shining my uniform shoes, and that, of course, is with a cake of polish that comes in a can, and that polish is black. White polish is different, a liquid in a bottle, and requires its own pristine buffing cloth. I found those shoes in the boys' department at Stone and Thomas. They were absolutely identical to the ones sold in the girls' department, and I was amazed that Stone and Thomas had got away with it. When I wore those saddle shoes, I was wearing girls' shoes, but nobody had to know that, did they?

Putting white polish on them was a magic ritual, as was walking in them — in the rain, in the twilight, across the Suspension Bridge over to town and back again.

This scene is like a pause in the narrative, but I can't leave it out. Polishing saddle shoes is difficult; you have to be careful not to get the black into the white or the white into the black. In this state of liminality, balanced on the edge between childhood and adolescence, the pain is sometimes so intense that I feel like I'm being eviscerated, but then, at the most unexpected times, the mystery is not a barrier but a bridge. Alone, balanced between day and night, between rain and twilight, with black-and-white saddle shoes on the window sill, I have no sense of ownership of this scene, but I can't say that I'm detached from it either. During these elusive moments of relief, "like a girl" is not something I would ever trade for a simpler, more ordinary life. I know that if I can never find the perfect story for me, I will have to write it myself.

*part V*

# BEAT

**1**

THE SPEEDOMETER NEEDLE was hovering at 130. I could see it clearly because I was jammed into the middle of the front seat between the driver — my buddy, Tom — and another boy whose name I don't remember. Three more boys were in the back. This was long before the era of seat belts. All of us were sixteen. "I wonder where the top end is on the old man's Buick," Tom had said. Sometime or other. A while back. God knows when. We were out on the River Road at midnight looking for that top end. We'd been drinking beer, Scotch, rye, gin, and bourbon — sometimes all of them dumped into one glass — and we were loud-mouthed reeling stupid dumb-ass staggering pissed-out-of-our-minds blind drunk. I'd been in that state often enough by then to get a good sense for it, so I figured I was close to passing out. I took a good slug from the fifth of bourbon and shoved it over to Tom. He tilted it back and gulped it down like Coke. I watched the speedometer needle float just a hair beyond that magic number — a record, the fastest I'd ever gone in my life. Sweat in my eyes, my whole body shaking with excitement, I was *there*, goddamn it, doing 130. I began to giggle hysterically. "Floor the fucker," I yelled.

"It *is* floored," Tom yelled back. It was the best joke we'd ever heard. We howled.

UNLIKE THE FANTASY FOLK who populate my grade-school stories — the ballerinas, Francophones, gun-toting gals, and sinister assassins — characters who resembled real people were beginning to appear in my high-school stories, along with bits of my own experience, but all of it transformed into fiction. Not long after it happened, I wrote an alternate version of that midnight run into a fifty-page "novel" called *Live for the Night*. I can date it to my junior year in high school by the song that opens it — "Over and Over," Bobby Day's hit tune from 1958. When my protagonist, Evan Carlyle, is listening to it, he's still living at home with his parents, but, within the first few pages, he does what I longed to do all through high school — announces to his mother that he's moving out to become a writer. She tries to talk him out of it, doesn't succeed, and he finds himself a ratty apartment in Center Wheeling. We're never told where his money's coming from — largely because I didn't have a clue. He spends his time writing beat poetry and hanging out with Alex Warner — a hard-drinking, fast-driving, bad-ass garage mechanic who represents my ideal West Virginia boy.

We pulled out and were on the River Road.
It was a little after midnight by my watch.

Alex flipped on the radio. I noticed for the first time it was a mobile ham set tuned to police calls. Up through the holy state of West Virginia we listened to them. The speedometer made me uncomfortable. It hovered around 90 on the average, slid down to 60 for the curves, and up to 110 on the straightaways. There was very little activity on the road, but we passed a few cars so fast they seemed to be barreling for all they were worth in reverse. Red headlights, almost instantly yellow lights moving alongside us, just as quickly gone, and receding headlights in the rearview. Alex was not reckless, he merely moved; he took the curves carefully, and though the tires screamed like banshees, we made every one.

"She moves pretty fast," I hazarded.

"Hell, man," said Alex with one of his rare chuckles, "we're not even in fourth."

We had just entered a straightaway inclined sharply upward to a hillcrest. He moved into fourth and floored it. With fascination I watched the speedometer climb — 100, 120, 130, 140 — at about 153 it seemed to reach its ceiling. Then we hit the crest and started down the other side. 160, 165 — the windows were open and the roar was so terrific I couldn't have heard Alex if he'd shouted. 170 was all it got; he saw curves coming, shifted into third, braked it sharply, and we were down to a more comfortable 90 by the time we hit them. He broke into the curve and accelerated out to the wild bellow of the tires. I was dripping with sweat; my shirt was soaked and stuck to my back and arms.

"Now you can tell me she moves if you want," he said and laughed. I had known him for two months, but it was the first time I had ever heard him laugh. It was a sound of pure joy, bubbling up from inside him, and in that instant I had a single brilliant insight into Alex Warner's life. When you live keyed up to danger, to some high point of experience, ordinary life seems tame. I knew now what the blank expression Alex always wore was; it was boredom.

YEARS AFTER we'd left high school behind, a friend told me that I'd been "very feminine" when I'd first showed up at Linsly. "You knew that, didn't you?" he said. I suppose that I did know it, but not the full extent of it.

I'd never forgotten my puzzlement when my mother had told me that I stood like a girl, talked like a girl, but if that's how my mother had seen me, other people must have seen me like that too.

"Protective coloration" is a term we learned in eighth-grade biology, and we made a joke of it, applied it to each other — the ability to blend in, to vanish into a group — and one of the most significant things I acquired in military school was a good solid layer of protective coloration. At first I wasn't intentionally imitating other boys; it was more a matter of being soaked in boy culture and adapting accordingly. Some boys couldn't adapt. They were teased and bullied mercilessly, and I badly wanted not to be one of them, so, by the time I got to high school, I was deliberately pursuing a hyper-masculine image. That meant considering every detail of how I dressed, how I moved, how I talked, and what I said.

We had our own private boy talk that we would never in a million years use in front of girls or adults. I jotted some of it down in my notebooks. We punctuated damn near every sentence with "fuck," referred to ourselves collectively with the word our teachers used for us, "gentlemen," but said with irony. We addressed each other as "boy," called each other a "load," short for a "load of shit." We had to be careful with the dire slur "faggot" because it could easily start a fight, but we yelled "queer" at each other with monotonous regularity. Feminine boys were labeled as sweet and edible — "candy," "candy-ass," "cupcake," "creampuff." The ability to trade insults was highly valued, and the best of them were recycled until everyone had heard them and got a good laugh — one-upping someone with, "bounce up and bite me, big boy," or calling someone "a needle-petered bug fucker."

Some of the boys policed gender down to the smallest detail. One afternoon we were lying in prone position in riflery class, taking turns shooting at the paper targets at the end of the hall. I was lying in such a way that my pants had ridden up, exposing my ankles. "Nice socks," a classmate said, reaching over and snapping the tops of them, and a low and smutty snicker passed around the hall. We were in uniform so of course my socks were black, but I was wearing them the way I'd done since I'd been five — rolled down neatly one turn, the way girls wore their socks. Until that moment I'd never thought about it. If this incident was as trivial as it should have been, why am I remembering it so vividly sixty years later?

WHAT ORIGINALLY attracted me to the great god Hemingway — "Papa," as he was known by then — was his emphatic masculinity — as Nabokov wickedly put it, that "bells, bulls, and balls" crap. I read every word Hemingway had ever written and thousands of the words that had been written about him. Papa was one of the world's great self-promoters, and the legend he'd created sucked me right in. I knew all about the wars, the plane wrecks, the boxing matches, the deep-sea fishing. I loved the Hemingway code — that a man keeps his mouth shut and gets on with it — loved Papa's nerve-shattered soldiers, battered boxers, and washed-up bullfighters who never lose their courage. Unlike the critics, I didn't think that the protagonist of *Across the River and Into the Trees* was a gassy old wind-bag full of shit; I thought that he was a mature man full of hard-won wisdom. You couldn't buy bullfight posters in Wheeling, so I painted my own and hung them on my walls — the ballerinas were emphatically gone by then, along with my gender-neutral clothing — and I pinned Papa's picture to my bulletin board so he could stare at me with those sad all-knowing eyes that could never be defeated. From somewhere in the Nick Adams stories I learned that you had to carry a knife to keep the queers off you, so I bought a switchblade in the pawnshop and carried it for years.

Papa had won the Nobel Prize. "Writing, at its best, is a lonely life," he'd said in his acceptance speech. The writer "does his work alone and if he is a good enough writer he must face eternity, or the lack of it, each day." *Face eternity* — wow, I thought, that's the writer's true calling. "A writer," Papa said, "is driven far out past where he can go, out to where no one can help him," and that was where I wanted to go too, sailing off into that uncharted and dangerous distance. Out there, in my splendid isolation, I would prove my courage by doing exactly what Hemingway had done so famously. I would attempt to write "one true sentence."

I'm not sure what *true* meant for Hemingway, but I know what it meant to me — it meant *real*. Trying for real, I included a sex scene in *Live for the Night*. Evan is invited into bed by a friend's sister:

> Sweat was rolling off me in torrents. Her studied casualness made me nervous as a cat. I got my wallet out of my pocket to get a safe, finished undressing, took several slugs of the booze, and got in bed with her. The streetlight shining through the drawn blind gave me just enough light to work by, but not enough to make me feel uncomfortable.
>
> We petted a while, then I undressed her and ran my hands up and down her naked body. I kissed her a few times, tongue in her mouth, but then couldn't wait any longer. She certainly wasn't a passive lover! She dug her heels into the bed, arched her back, and swung her pelvis up to meet me. We both went wild. I was exhausted afterwards and slept with my arms around her.

Those two paragraphs gave me the fits. Detailed, realistic descriptions of sex never appeared in '50s fiction, so all I had to go on was my imagination, and that scene was written by a seventeen-year-old who certainly didn't carry a safe around in his wallet and had never gone any farther with a girl than a prolonged French kiss.

When I slid over the climactic moments with, "We both went wild," I knew perfectly well that I was cheating.

## 2

SOMETIME EARLY IN MY TEENS my mother had delivered one of her obligatory prepared speeches that embarrassed her so intensely she could scarcely get the words out. It was excruciating for both of us. She stammered and hesitated, told me yet again how hard it was trying to be both a mother and a father to me. "A man has needs," she said eventually. It took me a while to figure out what on earth she was talking about. A woman of my mother's generation saw a man's sexual needs as an uncontrollable organic pressure analogous to the need to urinate. He didn't really have any choice in the matter. She understood this, she said, but she just wanted me to know that when I had to satisfy *my* needs, I should go to a prostitute rather than getting a nice girl in trouble.

I was flabbergasted. It wasn't that I didn't know what she meant—it simply didn't apply to me. I was obsessed with girls just as much as any other boy, but I didn't want what my friends wanted — "Hey, man, how far did you get? Did you get in her pants?" I never tried to take off a girl's bra, feel her breasts, or sneak my fingers up between her legs. Real boys wanted to fuck girls, and I kept thinking that if I was a real boy, that's what I should want too — and I had to pretend that I did so the guys wouldn't think I was queer. But that isn't what

I wanted. I didn't have a low sex drive; what I felt was fiery, urgent, and unrelenting, but — as odd as it might seem — all I wanted to do with girls was talk to them, hold their hands, and kiss them.

Because I was what most boys were not and all girls were supposed to be — a good listener — I made friends with a series of girls who must have regarded me as something like a male girlfriend. They told me about their lives and loves and dreams and problems, which was invaluable for the future novelist but didn't do much for my sex life. I felt deprived at the time, but now, looking back, I feel blessed. They must have seen me as enough like a girl that they could tell me their secrets. One of them gave me advice I should have taken. "Keith," she said, "you don't have to work so hard to be a boy."

But they weren't *all* Platonic buddies. Lots of girls wanted to kiss me just as much as I wanted to kiss them. Some I dated, and some I didn't, and now the old trickster memory has conjured up one in particular. I haven't thought about her in years. I'm not talking about a few minutes of kissing. I'm talking about sitting in my mother's old beat-to-shit Dodge on a smoldering summer's afternoon when the whole world sings with locusts, parked on a dirt road all the way to hell and gone, kissing from roughly two in the afternoon to dinner time.

I was seventeen. She was somebody's little sister — a tall scruffy skinny girl with short dark hair, a lean tomboy face, a spray of freckles across her nose, and brown eyes like mine. She was wearing a sleeveless white blouse with a bra under it, camp shorts, and a pair of those girls' white sneakers with the pointed toes that were fashionable at the time. She had shaved her long legs recently and rubbed suntan lotion on them so they gleamed in the afternoon light. "Androgynous" is a term that was years away from being available, but that's what she was — exactly the kind of boy-girl I had wanted to be during my pink shirt period.

I didn't attempt to remove an article of her clothing. We sat side by side and never touched each other *down there*. Our mouths were the primary actors. We chewed each other's earlobes, nibbled each other's lips and licked them, kissed each other's eyelids, neck, and cheeks, clung to each other. We took time out occasionally to breathe, to gaze into each other's eyes, but we always returned to the heart of the matter — the Holy French Kiss. What I'm talking about is sexual arousal for its own sake — a technique that has sometimes been recommended by the odd religious sect. I think it's easier for a girl to do that sort of thing for hours than it is for a boy — although I can't swear to it. From my own experience, I can tell you, however, that if you're a boy, and if you can keep on going through a nasty barrier of frustration, you'll leave all frustration behind, as I did, to end up in a state of bliss somewhat higher than the highest angels. This bit of deadpan prose is my attempt at a poem in praise of that girl whose name I don't remember. You were lovely. Thank you.

BILLY AND BECKY were only with us for a few years. When I was fifteen, our extended family broke apart. We'd been living in old Aunt Deal's house, and she went into a nursing home. My mother and grandmother and I moved into an apartment on Virginia Street. My bedroom had its own balcony, and I paced up and down there, staring down at the rain-smeared pavement — that's the nostalgic image that persists — and argued with the characters in my mind.

Becky graduated from high school and went to college in Texas, aided, the best I can remember, by scholarships and some help from relatives on her mother's side. I'm not sure where Uncle Bill was by then. I didn't give a shit about him or what he was doing — as he drifted from job to job, fired from one and finding another, floating on down the river, working in seedier and seedier hotels where he got to play the drunk on the night shift — but he ended up far down the river somewhere, maybe in Marietta, making enough money to pay the rent on a cheap ratty little apartment on the south end of the Island. Billy moved in there and became the only teenager I knew who lived alone.

Billy had a television set, and we didn't. Even though it was the crappiest TV I'd ever seen, he and I sat in front of it for hours, fooling with the rabbit ears. Some nights we couldn't make out much more than the suggestion of shapes in a deluge of snow, but we'd watch anyway — cop shows, mysteries — and then cook ourselves cheeseburgers, two boys without parents, alone in an apartment like a couple of the characters from one of the stories I was writing. Left to his own devices, he could do anything he damned well pleased, and some of the things he did were a little odd. He'd always wanted to know what dog food tasted like, so he bought a can, made it into patties, and fried it. I declined to taste it. He said it wasn't too bad, but he wasn't tempted to do it again. He couldn't afford to see a dentist, so he cleaned his teeth with Ajax, rubbing it into them with his index finger. His teeth were very white.

Walking into Billy's apartment one night, I discovered that he had acquired, by five-finger discount, a good half-dozen speakers that had formerly been attached to poles at the drive-in movie theater. Knowledgeable in the industrial arts, he'd wired them up everywhere — all the way down the hall and even in the bathroom. When Billy turned on the radio, his whole damn apartment became one huge speaker. I thought that was really cool, particularly in that it had cost him nothing but his time.

Billy was the perfect audience for my tales of "experiencing life." I drank myself into insensibility every chance I got, barfed up my guts on street corners and roadsides, never in anybody's car but once, alas, down at Fish Creek, inside my buddy's tent. I passed out in bars, in hallways, in mysterious unknown rooms, and once on a classmate's suburban front lawn, to awaken, hungover beyond belief in a murky dawn with the dew falling on me. I walked home across the Suspension Bridge one hot Sunday afternoon so loaded that the only thing that kept me from passing out was the sensation of my feet hitting the pavement; I felt every step as a shudder banging my rear teeth as I careened through a world that was as golden as bourbon — an enormous overheated overstuffed stupefied incomprehensible fuzz. Drunk, I annoyed other boys into wanting to pound me out but then, giggling and hanging onto their shirt fronts, talked them out of it. Drunk, I bailed out of the back of a moving pickup truck and was surprised at how hard the pavement came up to meet me.

When I experienced 130 miles per hour, I told Billy all about it — and about the other things I did that now strike me as the height of lunacy. In Elm Grove there's a lovely piece of engineering called "the S Bridge," shaped just the way its name implies. Whenever I got drunk enough to want to try it again, I'd drive my mother's old Dodge out there and see how fast I could shoot it across that goofy bridge. The bald tires were actually an asset because they helped with the slide I needed when I stomped on the brakes. The trick was to slide the middle of the bridge and pull out at the last minute — as I did a number of times, occasionally pinging my right rear quarter panel.

I didn't save my bursts of speed for the S Bridge but drove the twisty roads of the Ohio Valley like a lightning bolt from a Superman comic — changing lanes on the slightest impulse, grinning at the sound of somebody's brakes screaming behind me. I drag-raced other guys from school one night on the quiet streets of Woodsdale; my mother's machine wasn't built for that kind of work, and I lost every race, but at least I could tell Billy I'd done it. A girl I was dating said she could hardly wait to learn to drive — she wasn't sixteen yet — so I pulled over and said, "Okay, drive." She took off in a series of rabbit jumps, then sent us careening off the road and into a farmer's field while I sat in the passenger's seat and howled with laughter. I enjoyed "parking" in front of brick walls by approaching them at sixty and then braking at the last possible moment; if I'd timed it right, I'd hit the wall just hard enough to slam me forward into the steering wheel, then back into my seat — hey, kicks, man. My mother was working at Interstate Trucking then, and one of the drivers who'd caught my act in downtown Wheeling said, "Tell that son of yours if he keeps on driving like that, he ain't gonna live long."

### 4

I'D ALWAYS TAKEN my cousin Billy for granted — was sure that I knew him all the way to the bottom — but the older he got, the more he surprised me. Without bothering to tell anybody about it, he'd switched himself out of the industrial arts program at Wheeling High and into the college prep one, did so well that he'd become a member of the National Honor Society. He'd acquired a whole crop of new friends, become the head athletic manager at the school — popular enough to get himself elected as president of the Hi-Y. He took a lovely girl, a year older, to the Junior-Senior prom, and I have a picture of him wearing Buddy Holly glasses and the emblematic "white sport coat with a pink carnation." He looks as elegant as his dad did back in the days of easy money.

I walked in one evening and found him reading Herodotus, a beautifully bound volume with uncut pages that he'd bought by mail order — a collectors' item, the publisher promised. I have no idea what it cost, but whatever it was, Billy would have been taking money from his food allowance to pay for it. "Herodotus?" I said. "When the hell did you start reading Herodotus?"

He shook his head. "I don't know. I just like this stuff. I'm going to be a book collector."

Billy as a book collector? I had a hard time with that one. Who was this interesting guy who'd replaced my cousin?

Frank, a buddy from school, had turned me into a cave explorer — a "spelunker," we loved to say. West Virginia abounds in caves, and Frank and I had plumbed the depths of every one of them in the Wheeling area. Some other kids — not real spelunkers like us — told us that they'd seen what might have been a human body in a large cave just on the other side of the river. It had looked like the decayed remnants of a man, and after the first glance, they hadn't stuck around to study it. Frank and I had already been in that cave system, several times. "There's no body in there," he said, and that was that.

But I wanted to have a look for myself — well, maybe not *entirely* by myself. I took Billy with me.

He had never been in a cave before, but it didn't seem to bother him. Of course I'd read up on spelunking and had acquired all the proper equipment, starting with multiple light sources — acetylene torches, flashlights with fresh batteries, candles and matches as a backup. Billy was just as keen on finding that decaying corpse as I was. We imagined ourselves being written up in the *Wheeling News Register* — WHEELING YOUTHS FIND BODY. Because it was his first time, we had to go through the obligatory exercise in which you turn out every light and wait as your eyes keep fighting to see something — anything — and fail. Billy was just as impressed as I wanted him to be. "Jesus, it's dark!"

That cave system had two levels, and we explored both of them — every twist, turn, and cranny. I was much smaller than he was, so he waited, calling out to me from time to time, while I crawled to the end of passages so narrow I could barely work my shoulders through them. We were in there for hours. When we reemerged into the daylight, we could attest to the fact that there was no dead body in that damned cave. What those other boys must have seen, we decided, was a particular formation of stalagmites not far from the entrance. Those idiots had gone in there with nothing but candles; in that flickering light, that formation could very well have looked like the shape of a dead man.

"You like spelunking?" I asked my cousin.

"Oh, yeah." We explored several more caves together. It had dawned on me by then that Billy had turned into a friend of mine.

BEFORE I TURNED EIGHTEEN and received the magical Draft Card that would admit me to any bar in Wheeling, I made a lot of wine. As it did so often with so many things, the Ohio County Public Library assisted me in my efforts. Grapes were obvious, but it seemed that you could ferment damned near anything. I even tried milk because that's what they did in Mongolia — the curds float to the top, and you can scoop them off and get a clear white wine that's not half bad — but I discovered that if speed of delivery is what you're looking for, then what you need is potatoes. Lickety-split, in a week to ten days, potatoes can transform themselves from vegetable to alcohol. Under the cover of darkness and rain, Billy and I helped ourselves to several large aluminum beer barrels that had been conveniently left out for us at the back of a saloon, carried them down to his place, washed them out in the bathtub, and crammed them full of potato mash — that is, chopped up and boiled potatoes mixed with sugar and yeast. We covered them with cheesecloth and waited. Eventually we got what we wanted. Boy, did it taste like shit, but it worked just fine.

My senior year in high school, Billy's junior year, we had ourselves one hell of a party in his apartment. I invited some of my classmates. Many of us had turned eighteen by then, so we had plenty of beer, and some of the guys had raided the old man's liquor cabinet, so we had rye and bourbon, and, of course, gallons of our foul, thick, white, sludgy potato wine — the perfect thing for end-of-the-world chugging contests — and we got beautifully polluted, treated the neighborhood to the likes of Chuck Berry through Billy's multiple speaker system, then moved on to braying out the Linsly Alma Mater and other venerable drinking songs — and had the honor of being visited by the Wheeling Police Department at two in the morning. Big, burly, pissed-off guys with guns hammered at the door. Once we opened it, they proceeded to throw us bodily down the stairs. "Where the hell you from?" one of them yelled at me. "Moundsville," I said, inspired.

"Well, get your sorry ass back there."

I wandered the streets in a happy daze for a while, then went back to help Billy clean up the mess. Now I thought that maybe my cousin wasn't just a friend of mine. He seemed to be turning into one of my best friends.

5

MANY OF MY FICTIONAL PEOPLE vanished almost as soon as I'd created them, but Alex Warner and Evan Carlyle wouldn't go away. They matured right along with me, lived in various drafts of various stories over the years, became increasingly grounded in something resembling a real world, and eventually, as characters always do if they've got any juice to them, separated from me and took off on their own. The Dial Press published *Alex Driving South* in 1980. When I received the advance copy, I took the book out of its package, held it in my hands, sat down at my desk, and wept. I couldn't believe it. I'd been living with those guys for twenty-two years, and they'd finally made it into print.

Looking back now at the first appearance of Alex and Evan, I see that there are parts of *Live for the Night* I never developed because I perceived, quite rightly, that they were too ungrounded, melodramatic, and downright weird to preserve. Brenda Kovic is one of my recurrent ballet dancers. She runs her own dance studio in an unnamed town down the river from Wheeling. Like many of my characters, she has been infested by the worm of despair and asks herself the fatal question — *why bother to go on living?* When the characters in my high-school writing ask themselves that, there's only one thing that can save them — that is if somebody, anybody, *understands them.* But nobody understands Brenda, so she hangs herself. I seemed to see the act of suicide as presenting its own irrefutable argument. It certainly has that impact on Evan Carlyle:

I walked the streets for hours trying to take it
in. Then, suddenly, it came to me; I saw it all,
entire and complete. I knew how she had felt,
knew the feeling of the hand that had fastened
the knot.

Once Evan has experienced that flash of insight, that's the end of him; all he needs is a gun to blow his brains out. He gets one from Alex Warner, but Alex — canny fellow that he is — knows exactly what Evan is up to and gives him blanks. Evan goes home, sits down, raises the gun to his right temple, and pulls the trigger. Alex walks in right behind him and says, "Well, man, you committed the act, are you satisfied? I've got a box of live shells right here, so if you want to displace your brains, you can, but we're gonna have a little talk first, 'cause I sure as hell have a lot to say to you." Indeed he does. The story ends with Alex Warner's nine-page argument in favor of life.

IN THE STORIES I was writing, the action often stops dead so the characters can argue with each other. Sometimes I didn't bother with a story at all but went straight to the argument. I wrote more essays in high school than poetry or fiction, argued as only a teenager can — with a fiery, single-minded, utterly naïve vehemence as though I wanted to grab the reader by the throat and yell, "Listen to me, you idiot, *this is serious!*" My inner war of opposites had coalesced around two nodes. I shot back and forth between them like a shuttlecock.

On the one side there was the stuff generated in my mind from reading *On the Road* and *The Dharma Bums*. A shimmery pattern was coalescing around the Buddhism of Gary Snyder, D.T. Suzuki, and Alan Watts, around the Beat poetry of the unabashedly queer Allen Ginsberg. That side fit easily into the New Deal liberalism I'd sopped up as a child growing up in a union town with a mother who worked for a living. I wandered around in a beret, black sweater, torn jeans, and sandals, talked like a Kerouac character, and invited my friends back to my pad to drink Zen tea. When I was on that side, I argued that sex roles were not natural but the product of what I called "the environment," that the terms "masculine" and "feminine" were meaningless.

On the other side were good old Papa Hemingway, Ayn Rand of *The Fountainhead* and *Atlas Shrugged*, and, God help me, Friedrich Nietzsche — all of whom, at least in the way I was reading them, were pushing me toward that wacky far-right position we now call "Libertarian." When I was on that side, I had my hair buzzed down to Marine-recruit length, wore work shirts, baggy jeans, and motorcycle boots, and argued that feminism had rotted America to its very core, that, if we were to be saved from sinking further into the shame of utter degeneracy, women must once again become truly feminine and men truly masculine.

I wrote two stories with the same title — "The Downgoing" — each starring my version of Nietzsche's Superman. The title is borrowed from *Thus Spake Zarathustra*. Nietzsche's hero, his Superman, is feeling the plenitude of his wisdom, and he knows he must go down, go under — that is, into the world of men, below mankind, so that he can share his wisdom with humanity. The Superman is the savior, the enlightened being, the one filled with wisdom who will redeem the world — or at least that's the way I construed him, probably reading counter to Nietzsche's anti-Christian message, although it's hard not to see something of Christ in Zarathustra.

Written from the Beat-Buddhist side, my Superman is not a man at all but a Supergirl — Butch Carlyle. There had been plenty of girl protagonists in my juvenile fiction before her — it's as though whenever I wanted to give anyone a really serious problem to solve, I automatically picked a girl — but Butch is the first of my girl protagonists to speak in her own voice.

The minute I stopped writing about a girl in the third person, from the *outside*, and tried it in the first person, from the *inside*, all my earlier cartoon-like girls dropped away. Butch is not a wide-eyed innocent, nor a '50s teenage sexpot in a tight skirt, nor a tortured young ballerina, nor a tomboy who can beat the crap out of anybody, nor a cool private investigator with stiletto heels and a .45 in her purse. Butch is short, slightly plump, and, as she tells us, "pretty enough but no knockout." She's a beat poet living in an imaginary, nightmarish New York where even the rain is "putrescent," and I provide a three-page sample of her poetry — the style, cadence, vocabulary, and subject matter lifted straight from T.S. Eliot.

Butch has sex with her boyfriend — who looks suspiciously like Kerouac's Dean Moriarty — and with a few other guys, and, in two quick and elusive paragraphs, with another girl. "Sex," she says, "is the most beautiful and hallowed act on the face of the earth." I don't remember how I picked her first name, if I was aware of the connotations of "butch" and liked them, or if I simply wanted her to have a boyish name. That I gave her the same last name as *Evan* Carlyle — a character who was, at least initially, some version of myself — tells me how much I must have identified with her.

Butch, like somebody out of Kerouac, is heavy into booze and drugs. Eventually her lifestyle catches up to her. "You can't live as fast as we had been and not feel it. I couldn't hold a glass in my hand without the liquid spilling. I was jumpy and looked awful. I was dismal, I was tired, I was sad and lonely and melancholy and beat." Looking back on her life, she tells us that she had "plumbed the depths of despair and, in that way, had taken the sins of the world vicariously on my shoulders." I saw her as a Bodhisattva, a future redeemer of mankind, and imagined that she would — as I hoped that I would — become a compassionate, enlightened being.

I felt good writing from a girl's point of view, but I felt guilty about it too — and eventually stopped. It wasn't as though I thought that I had no right to be there. It was more that I couldn't imagine allowing anyone to *see me there*. I gave up on Butch and had another try at the Superman. This time he is very much a man:

Saul was a big man, built like a column of tempered steel. He was dark, dark with days and days of sun and wind and driving rain. His muscles were hard and strong, surrounding his body like iron. His hair was black, cut short in a crew cut, and he wore a beard and mustache, heavy and dark. His mouth, like the rest of his face, appeared to be cut from the granite he worked, while his eyes were smoldering black fire under thick and malignant brows. The tendons in his neck were hemp ropes, his veins stood out strongly in his blackened hands and arms, and his broad hard chest was covered with a mat of hair. Here was a man who could have been practically anything but what he was. On the street, you could have taken him for a fighter or a truck driver or a structural worker, yet this bull of a man with a weight lifter's shoulders and a sprinter's legs was a sculptor.

Behold the man! I'm laughing as I write this, but in high school I was deadly serious. When I tried to imagine men becoming "truly masculine," Saul is the first figure that came striding into my mind. Ayn Rand recommends selfishness as the finest of all human traits, and I was following her lead — Saul is a real prick. I told his story for only a few pages — stopping when I realized that I didn't like him at all — so

I'm not sure now what I might have planned for him. A war probably, because war is a man's work, and of course he would have to kill somebody — and in the end, a truly masculine man always gets the girl. From *Tap Roots* I had learned that if you have a rival in love, you simply fire a powerful charge, a large ball and two small ones, right between his eyes. What the no-good boys in the storage locker had told me had been crude and unsophisticated — you didn't actually have to *hit* a woman — because if you were truly masculine, then a woman would eagerly submit to you, as Morna submits to Keith Alexander. "I am as he wants me to be," she says, "and if the day ever comes when I am not, he will break me across his will and make me as he wants me to be."

6

WHILE I WAS WRITING about "truly masculine" Saul, I was also still secretly reading fashion magazines, and I used those images of beautifully dressed girls to create an elaborate fantasy I told myself as I was going to sleep. This fantasy was not a sexual one — it gave me intense pleasure, but it didn't turn me on. I would dress myself like a stylish young lady and then do something perfectly ordinary — walk over to town, go to a movie, go shopping — and I would look exactly like a girl except that I wouldn't actually be one. And here was the best part — in the world I was creating *nobody cared because it was all perfectly ordinary.* This was, of course, not the kind of fantasy that a "truly masculine" man should be having, so I told no one about it and loathed myself for having it.

Somewhere in the midst of stewing in my adolescent juices, I also tossed into the cauldron Mary Renault's first novel set in ancient Greece, *The Last of the Wine.* I'd been reading Plato, had turned into an exercise nut, cultivating my healthy mind in my healthy body, asking myself the Socratic question, "How should I live?" so it was the perfect book for me. Both Socrates and Plato appear as characters — which excited me no end — but at the core is a gay love story, the first I'd ever read. I strongly identified with Alexias, the younger boy, the slender delicate runner. In Renault's version of ancient Greece, boys, when they come of age, are regarded much the way we regarded girls in the '50s — as exquisite prizes to be won.

A seemingly trivial incident from when I'd been thirteen had got stuck in my memory in a persistent way that told me it wasn't trivial at all. One day at school during lunch break, an older boy had grabbed me, shoved me in front of his friends, and said — and this was not meant to tease me, embarrass me, or make me feel bad; I could tell that he meant it as a compliment — "Look at his skin. Doesn't he have the most beautiful complexion you ever saw?"

I'd never thought of my complexion as particularly beautiful. I hadn't begun to grow hair on my face yet, had never suffered from the skin blemishes that made the lives of other boys miserable, and as I stood there, I thought, well, yeah, I guess I do have a nice complexion. A half a dozen boys were staring at me — they were all *much* older than I was — and I felt myself flush. I wasn't naïve about what was going on. All of us knew something about homosexuality — being queer, we would have said — but the way our culture was constructed, it was simply not a possibility for us. If it had been, that boy could never have thrust me forward so impulsively to be admired by his friends. But I knew something that he didn't know, something that he would never have admitted even to himself — that he found me sexually attractive.

I was surprised at my own reaction. This was at the height of my pink shirt period, and I *wanted* to be beautiful, so I wasn't the least bit alarmed, ashamed, or embarrassed. Talking didn't seem to go with the role I'd been thrust into, so I didn't say a word, simply stood there — aware of being on display — and waited for the boys to finish looking at me. If that incident had led anywhere, I would have been horrified, but it didn't. I'd felt safe the entire time, and it had been just enough. Reading *The Last of the Wine* brought that memory back and, as we would say now, contextualized it. However much I might have wished it wasn't true, I had to admit that the thought of being a beautiful boy courted by adoring older boys was something I found intensely attractive.

Anything to do with homosexuality in the 1950s carried such a fearsome emotional charge that it might be difficult for younger readers today to feel the full impact of it. In 1953 President Eisenhower had signed an executive order prohibiting homosexuals from working for the federal government. They were thought to be security risks because they were susceptible to blackmail, and thousands were fired. In the mainstream media they were referred to as "sexual perverts." Senator Joe McCarthy, that most wretched of men, hadn't only been going after supposed communists; he'd been going after gays too, eagerly assisted by J. Edgar Hoover, the head of the FBI. It was frequently suggested that gays were un-American and somehow naturally attracted to communism. Homosexuality was regarded by the medical community as a mental illness, and sodomy was a felony in every state in the union; in some states you could do years at hard labor for committing it. Absolutely nobody was out, and being outed could cost you your job, your family, your social standing — dammed near everything.

I can't claim that when I was in high school I was fully aware of all of this stuff going on, but I was aware of some of it, and I was certainly aware of the dire emotional tone in the culture. Just as under the despicable Jim Crow laws, if one drop of African blood made you black, then in such a terrified climate, one drop of queer could make you a faggot. All males then, those with any common sense, were ceaselessly engaged in the most meticulous self-scrutiny to make sure that they weren't giving off even the faintest suggestion of that one drop. Looking inside myself, I found more than one drop. What was I supposed to do about that? Trying to learn how to be a man by reading Nietzsche, Ayn Rand, and Ernest Hemingway is not something that I would recommend to anyone.

At the time I had only the vaguest notion of what my internal arguments circled around, although I could feel the dead weight at the center. If there is no one like you anywhere in the world, and if you can't even find anyone like you portrayed *in fiction* — and I couldn't — you are left in a fairly untenable position in terms of getting on with your life and living it. Outside, I was presenting to the world a standard-issue teenage boy, but inside, I might as well have been a two-headed calf born in the dark of the moon.

HERE ARE TWO FRAGMENTS of memory that I have never, before now, placed side by side to see how they might inform each other. Sometime in the fall of my junior year I was riding in a car with my buddies, rock 'n' roll blasting from the radio, and moving too fast — that goes without saying — when the driver suddenly turned, tires screaming, and shot us off into one of Wheeling's pretty, tree-lined residential suburbs. We went barrel-assing up a steep hill and passed two girls walking. They weren't children. In those days you could tell, just by looking at their clothes, how old girls were, and these were old enough to date. They were holding hands — something that an adult did with a child, or a man with a wife, or a boyfriend with a girlfriend, but no one else was supposed to do. One of my buddies leaned out the car window and yelled, "Lezzies!" The girls dropped each other's hands as suddenly as if they'd been stung.

That incident hurt me. I thought it was cruel and unfair of my buddy to have yelled at those girls, but it was more than that. I felt that something precious, tender, and infinitely valuable had been sullied.

At roughly the same time, I got to play that scene from the other side. I was walking across the Suspension Bridge with a boy a few years younger than I was. We stepped onto the bridge and started across. With no preamble whatsoever, he took my hand and held it.

I became instantly alert to the dangers of the world, all of my antenna going up, as though the hills and the river had suddenly opened a thousand eyes. I was ready, prepared in my mind, to hear a jackass voice braying out of a car. If we were to run into a pack of boys who offered to kick our teeth down our throats, then I was going to have to fight — me, who'd never been in a serious fight in his life — because I'd just found my line in the sand. Nothing would have made me let go of that boy's hand or deny the spontaneous affection that had made him reach out to take my hand. I wanted to protect him. The world would let him know soon enough that you don't hold hands with another boy, but he was not going to learn it from me.

IT'S HARD FOR ME to tell how much of my high school writing was driven by genuine feelings I was having at the time and how much by my attempts to imitate writers I admired. I can't remember suicide as a major theme in any of the books I was reading, yet I wrote about it as though it were a contagious disease as common as the flu. A good half dozen of my characters think seriously about it, one attempts it, and two others actually do it. I don't remember feeling suicidal during my high-school years, and I do know what it feels like because I was suicidal later on — in my twenties.

Suicidal is where you arrive after you've passed through the far side of despair, and then it can be a flat, emotionless state in which you ruminate obsessively, in considerable realistic detail, on how you're going to do it. What stopped me each time was a simple proposition. If you really *are* at the bottom of the pit, if you really *don't* give a shit, you have become curiously invulnerable, and then previously unimaginable things have suddenly become possible — and some of those new possibilities are bound to be a hell of lot more interesting than killing yourself. That's precisely the argument Alex gives Evan at the end of *Live for the Night*.

Throughout my adolescence I dreamed that I was infested with insects, and I actually did get infested. I'd been swimming in the river — well, not swimming, that's too strong a word. Neither Billy nor I had ever learned to swim. We could dog paddle, and could tread water, and that was about it, but both of us pretended we could swim because we were boys and we were supposed to know how. I don't remember who was with me, but I do remember the free-wheeling kick of the beer and the Van Gogh stars spiraling over my head. I'd never been in the river, but my buddies were going in, so why the hell shouldn't I? I stayed close to shore. And while I was in the river for the only time in my life, something crawled into my left foot and decided to live there — in the concavity between my ankle and my heel — a small circular loop of foreign tissue that looked like a worm. It was a parasite, I thought. That was my personal diagnosis. It never occurred to me to consult with our family doctor.

I had a fencing foil that belonged to my cousin Billy. The cork tip had come off, revealing a small flat disk of steel. Alone in my bedroom, I heated the disk in a candle flame until it glowed red and then used it to burn that parasite out of my foot. Yes, it did hurt, but saying so is somehow beside the point. I had to do it slowly, gradually, reheating the fencing foil time after time. Whatever that thing was, that foul presence living in me, I knew that I had to *burn it out*. I kept at it until every trace of it was gone. The wound didn't scar; it healed cleanly and quickly, just as I'd known it would — because I'd *cauterized* it — and all that's left of it now is a small white irregularity no bigger than a match head. I didn't think that what I'd done was a big deal. I've never bothered to tell this story before. Like a Hemingway character, I'd simply done something a man should do — because it needed to be done — and a man doesn't talk about such things afterwards. I remember willing myself to breathe slowly and deeply. I remember soaking my shirt with sweat. I don't remember the pain, but I remember the silence.

### 7

ON AUGUST 13, 1960, I was sitting in the music room at the Ohio County Public Library with my best friend, Dick Webb, playing a game we'd made up. Each of us would select a record from the library's collection for the other to identify. If we couldn't nail it down to a specific composer, then we tried to place it in its historical period and explain our reasons. I can't remember what Dick picked for me, although I think it was one of those tinkly Italians I hadn't got straight yet — Vivaldi or Scarlatti. Dick was in music school, and it was getting harder to find composers he couldn't identify, so I'd chosen a piece by someone I thought might be obscure enough to stump him — Ernest Bloch. After only a few bars, Dick said, "Oh, that's Jewish," and then the orchestration and harmonic structure told him that it was modern. "No earlier than the '20s," he said, and he was right, but he'd never heard Bloch before. I was pleased.

We stepped out of the library into the glory of summer, the rare kind of day that came to us in the Valley sometimes like a gift — when the air pollution blew away, when it wasn't too hot or humid, when the sky was the clear lucent blue of dreams. We walked through town, on our way back to my place on the Island, and I remember being fully aware — as I wasn't often then — of being young. I was eighteen years old, out of high school and still savoring it. I felt in tune with my body — fit and fresh and ready for anything, ready to go off into the world. I remember what I said to Dick, and I remember when I said it. We were walking across the Suspension Bridge. It was a simple enough thought, a true one that had never occurred to me before I'd read it in a magazine. "It's great to be happy," I said, "but most of the time it's something we remember. We look back and say, 'Oh, I was happy.' The best thing of all is to know that you're happy when you are happy . . . and I'm happy *right now.*"

We walked the rest of the way across the bridge and continued on up Virginia Street to the apartment where I lived with my mother and grandmother. I was already thinking about how that wonderful afternoon would fade into the cool blue of evening. We would have dinner and sit on my balcony and talk for a while. Then we'd walk back to town and drink a few beers. I couldn't imagine anything more pleasant. In a month I would be leaving home. By God, I was ready to leave.

We walked up the stairs to the apartment. I can still see the door and the landing — the golden light with motes in it. As we stepped inside, we were met by my cousin, Becky. She was going to school in Texas, but she'd been home all summer. She was crying. I felt a sudden cold constriction of the heart.

"The police were just here," she said. "They told us that Billy's drowned in the river."

That was ridiculous of course. "What are you talking about?"

"The police were here. The police were *just* here. They said Billy was swimming in the river. There were two other kids with him. He got out too far or something. He got swept out in the current too far or something. He got swept away. They said he drowned in the river."

"No," I said, "that can't be right."

I couldn't talk anymore, couldn't say anything, but my mind kept on going, telling me that it wasn't possible. He could not have drowned in the river. They were going to have to — I didn't know what. Find him, that's what they were going to do. Somebody would have a boat.

Things came apart. All I have now are fragments — my memory shredded like confetti. I don't remember if Dick stayed for a while or if he went back to Martins Ferry right away. I don't remember talking to Becky or to my mother or my grandmother — although I must have. I remember that later that night, when I couldn't sleep, I was alone.

My uncle Bill came over to our place when he got the news. He badly needed a drink. My mother called an old friend of his who had underworld connections, and a bottle arrived in a taxicab. I could hear Bill roaming around the apartment, walking up and down the long hallway. Sometime in the night he came into my room. "I can't stop thinking of him out there in the river," he said.

"I keep thinking about Binky out there rolling around in the river."

I don't remember crying, not then, although I did later. The story came out in fragments and gradually assembled itself. Billy and two other boys — all three were seventeen — had been swimming in the river. They'd been just south of the railroad bridge near the channel buoy, in a part of the river where there was an underwater ledge. As long as they stayed over that ledge, they would have been close enough to the bottom to be able to touch down.

Billy had been drawn by the current and carried away from the underwater ledge and out into the deeper channel of the river. In that deep channel, the river runs fast. It would take an expert swimmer to swim across that channel, and even an expert swimmer would be swept downstream by it. It happened, the reports said, between 4:15 and 4:25 in the afternoon — exactly at the time when Dick and I had been sitting in the music room testing each other's musical knowledge. As Billy had been swept away by the current, and pulled off into the deep current, he'd begun to yell for help. He'd yelled for help the entire time he'd been drowning. A boat had been passing by, but people on the river were used to hearing kids yelling — horsing around, goofing off, pretending to drown — and they didn't pay any attention. The two other boys splashed to shore and ran straight to the Ohio Valley Yacht Club. That was where you went for help for trouble on the river, and everybody knew it.

The Yacht Club responded immediately, sent out boats and equipment from the fire department. They sent skin divers down into the river looking for Billy's body. They began dragging operations. At least ten boats were involved. By 8:30 in the evening, they moved search-lights in to help with the dragging operations. By ten o'clock that night, they discontinued dragging. I couldn't sleep. The only place I could possibly be was down by the river.

The next day one of my old classmates from Madison — one of the chatty girls who'd shared the first row with me in the first grade — was out with her family in a boat. I don't know if they were looking for Billy's body, but they found it. Their boat bumped into him. I couldn't stop playing the thought of Billy drowning — the moment when he was first going under and knew it, the moment when he'd first sucked in water instead of air. I played through the whole story — the panic, the burst of adrenaline, the will to live, the fight to live — but then what? I couldn't take it any further. It blotted out in me.

I was one of his pallbearers. My mother said, "Are you sure you want to do this? It's rough when it's one of your own." I didn't care how rough it was. I knew I had to do it.

The week before he died, Billy had been riding his bike and had taken a bad spill. He had cinders ground into his hands, had still been picking them out. In the funeral home, the cinders were still there. I could see them in his hands folded on his chest. Part of his face had been destroyed, and the funeral people had restored it with wax, molding in part of his lip on one side. They had done a reasonably good job — but I could still see that his face had been ruined. His coffin was in the same position in the same room where his mother's had been. I had never in my life cried as much as I did when I saw his body.

PEOPLE KEPT SAYING, "What was he doing out there in that river?" My grandmother must have asked that a hundred times. "He couldn't swim. He knew he couldn't swim. What was he doing out there in that river?"

I'd learned from Hemingway that a man doesn't talk about such things, a man just gets on with it, so that's what I tried to do, but I suffered from a soul-grinding survivor's guilt. It could have been me just as easily as him — even more easily. *Why him and* not *me?* My worst thought was that I'd always been the older one, the leader, so I might have aimed him down the path that would eventually kill him — but it was more complicated than that. We had been fellow members of the fucked-up white boys club. I knew perfectly well why he'd been out there in that river.

1955 WAS THE YEAR they built the Fort Henry Bridge across the Island. Billy and I were walking over to town to go to a show. We wanted to see how they were coming with the new bridge — if we could cross it yet — so we walked up to the point where they had fenced it off, put up signs saying: D A N G E R — N O  E N T R Y. We looked over the fence at the section that didn't have any flooring on it yet — a long span across the middle of the river. All that connected that span were steel girders slightly wider than the length of one of my feet turned sideways.

Both of us had seen *Rebel Without a Cause* — we'd been sitting side by side in the theater — but neither of us would have ever called the other chicken. We were too close for that. We weren't trying to impress each other. No one would ever know whether we'd done it or not, so the kids we wanted to impress were phantom kids. The best I can remember, it was simple. "Do you want to?" I said.

"Sure," he said.

Two boys with something to prove. A boy who had never believed himself to be a real boy, who often felt like a girl. A boy whose mother had died when he was seven, whose father was a drunk, whose father had abandoned him, who had almost put him in the Children's Home. We never talked about it, so I don't know what Billy thought. For me, it was what it always was. Any boy who was terrified of heights but who could walk across that empty space with nothing to walk on but those narrow steel girders, with *nothing to hold onto* — that boy had to be a man. We crawled under the fence. That part was easy.

The steel girders were slick and so were the leather soles of my dress shoes. I can't remember what Billy had on his feet. I started across first, and he walked behind me. I knew that I had to walk slowly and deliberately or I'd never make it. With each step I made sure that one foot was planted firmly on the girder. Then I moved the free foot around in a careful arc and placed it directly in front of the weight-bearing foot. Then I shifted my weight to the lead foot and did it again. After only a few steps, I got a whiff of the height, and I knew that I'd made the biggest mistake of my life. I didn't need to know that the middle of the Fort Henry Bridge is two hundred feet above the Ohio River. I could see that the fall would kill us.

I thought of going back, but Billy was right behind me. I was sure that if I tried to turn around, we'd both go over. I thought of getting down on my belly and crawling across, but I knew that if I tried to go from standing to kneeling to stretched out flat, I'd surely go over. I had started something I had to finish. I had to keep taking one more deliberate step and then one more after that. The height sucked at me through my eyes, and my legs started shaking.

I knew that if I allowed myself to see the height, I would die. My visitations had taught me something — those times when things came into my mind and buzzed, when the whole world turned yellow, when I had to fight to keep from screaming or crying. Walking across that emptiness was just like that. I needed to fill up every inch of my mind, so I built the multiplication tables into my footsteps. I breathed slowly and deeply. However many single steps it would take, that was how many it was going to take, and there was nothing I could do about it. I knew that I couldn't allow myself to think about it. I took one step at a time — five eights are forty, six eights are forty-eight, seven eights are fifty-six — and eventually I got to the fence on the other side.

I don't know what Billy did to focus himself. Maybe he simply followed me, and when I took a step, he took a step. We crawled under the fence and walked on into town and went to a movie. Afterward, as we started home, I said, "You want to go back across the Fort Henry Bridge?" We looked at each other and smiled. We didn't need to do it again. We walked home across the Suspension Bridge. Billy was twelve, and I was thirteen.

# part VI

# THE REST IS SILENCE

**1**

DURING THE LAST YEARS of my teens and well into my twenties, I was suicidal. My memories of that time are fragmented and elusive, but I know that I thought about suicide relentlessly and actually attempted it once — in a half-assed and half-hearted way. I can't remember exactly what happened — I was blind drunk — although I do remember waking up the next day, thinking, yep, that was a suicide attempt. I also avidly pursued suicide by accident, crawling deep into caves and mineshafts, climbing to the tops of water towers and tall buildings, getting totally pissed and trying to pick fights with people who would have slaughtered me, hanging out with sketchy people in dangerous places. I hitchhiked all over the Eastern United States, sometimes taking off on sudden impulse and more than once found myself standing by the side of the road god knows where as the traffic thinned out and the sun went down. I was chased on foot by the cops a couple of times, was thrown in jail for drunk and disorderly, was pounded out on the street and ended up in the hospital with a split lip and a concussion. I had learned from an early age that a distinguishing feature of men is their burning desire to drink, so I emulated my uncle Bill. I started out on beer but after a few years switched to bourbon; by the end, anything would do. I am fairly certain that if I'd had access to a gun, I wouldn't be here.

This book is a severely focused memoir, not my autobiography, and there is much that I'm intentionally leaving out, and that includes the quiet productive times. My life as a child and adolescent was generally happier than anything that I've written so far might imply, and more complex. I was blessed with good friends. I counted on them, and no matter how much of an asshole I was, they never let me down. I also kept learning new things that made me consider the possibility that I might actually have a future.

When I was nineteen, I visited New York for the first time. For years I had been imagining New York as the absolute center of the universe, so actually being there was exhilarating. I saw lots of foreign films, heard a folk singer or two, and studied the phone directory for any organization that listed itself as Buddhist. I connected with three of them. Each had an important lesson for me.

One was a Chinese Buddhist temple. The priest unlocked the building and showed me around. The main thing to see was a huge statue of the seated Buddha. The priest's English was rudimentary but plenty good enough to get the job done. "See flower?" he said. "Lotus. Very important to Buddha. Means beautiful flower grows out of shit."

The American Buddhist Academy was a hostel for Japanese Buddhist scholars visiting New York. When I rang the front doorbell, the gentleman in charge stepped outside to greet me, and he too had something he wanted to point out to me — another Buddha, this one a nearly life-sized figure standing by the door. "Buddha is green," he said. Yes, I could see that. The statue was very green, as green as jade. I nodded. "Not always green," he said. "Was at Hiroshima," and then he laughed.

My third visit was to an apartment building. I rang the bell, and someone buzzed to let me in — an American woman. At nineteen I would have seen anyone over forty as middle-aged, and that's all I remember about her. To my delight she was eating a fish head, complete with eye, on a bowl of rice, eating it with chopsticks, and I knew that I had come to the right place. For years I was sure that she was Ruth Fuller Sasaki — I don't know how I got that idea into my head — but now, checking online, I see that she could not possibly have been, so I don't know who she was and don't remember how she listed herself in the phone directory. To my further delight it turned out that she knew both Kerouac and Ginsburg, knew them personally, although she didn't think much of them — "They spend all of their time riding around New York in taxicabs."

She told me about taking part in a Buddhist ceremony in Japan, "The Fire Ceremony," and bragged that no Westerner could possibly sit all the way through it — but she had. I can't remember much of anything else she said, but she asked me if I knew how to sit zazen, and of course I didn't. "There's no time like the present," she said — I clearly remember the annoyance in her voice — and motioned for me to get down on the floor. My legs went fairly easily into a half lotus. She showed me how to hold my hands and what to do with my eyes, keeping them open but "soft," and she taught me how to count my breaths from one to ten. So there was my basic introduction to Zen meditation.

## 2

I CONTINUED TO THINK of myself as a writer, and when I was twenty-three, did what I had always promised myself I would do — completed the first draft of a novel. I don't remember why I chose Hamlet's last words for the title — *The Rest Is Silence* — maybe because I was sure that I would die soon and had only one book in me.

It's been years since I've looked at that manuscript, but I'm looking at it now. It's a strange document, a paste-up job — 278 pages clipped into a three-ring binder, fragments of my earlier writing taped in between stretches of new writing. A helpful friend using a red pen has corrected some of my erratic spelling, and I've edited the manuscript myself, using a black pen, moving clauses around, replacing phrases or words, scratching out the real names of places and substituting fictional ones. As a first attempt at a novel, it's rough as hell, a long way away from anything a publisher might want, but it gives me a clear insight into the mess that was in my mind when I wrote it.

It opens with a character from my high school stories, Alex Warner. He's driving, of course, and thinking of the curve in the road a half-mile ahead — "an egg-shaped back-tracking loop which describes the circumference of a ridge, a real ass kisser, the most dangerous piece of road from here to Herrod."

The approach was straight, marked with the understatement of a sign reading: C U R V E A H E A D — 15 M P H, then the road bent, blind, sharply to the right around the ridge. At the farthest segment of its parabola course, the turn had been mercifully widened beyond the normal two lanes, flanked with a guard rail which soil erosion had sunk to a mere hubcap high projection above the berm. Over the edge was a short drop, then a long rolling slope into the valley.

"I'll power slide the son of a bitch," thought Alex. "No lights ahead. Wet road. She'll slide, just get her out in time." Passing the road sign, he geared down to ninety. He touched the brake, watched the needle drop as he used up the last of the straightaway, then, at fifty, hit the clutch, downshifted to second, and kicked the brake, hard, cutting the wheel sharply to the right.

The car jerked around, sideways to the road, with tires screaming across the wet pavement. Alex cut the wheel back to hold his sideways course into the turn, let up on the brakes, and jammed down on the accelerator. The engine, out of gear, howled. The car swung wide around the turn, using both lanes, still sideways.

Just before the trajectory of the headlights aligned itself with the path of the road, Alex popped the clutch, and the rear tires spun tractionless. Then they caught, and their forward drive fought with the sideways line of force for control of the automobile. The car slid into the guard rail, flipped sideways off the road, and was airborne upside down. "Looks like I bought it," thought Alex.

For an instant which seemed ridiculously long there was near silence. Through the windshield Alex could see his headlights focused on precisely nothing. Then the car lit on the left side of the roof. The windshield exploded.

The diagonal of body directly to the left of Warner's head buckled to his shoulder. And the right door, ripped open by compression, carried by centrifugal force, spun off into the night.

The automobile slid down the hill on its roof, bounced off a crest of ground, and described another airborne sideways turn to land right side up, the tires ballooning and ripping away, then, the slope of the ground to help it, rolled over again. Alex counted four more complete revolutions before the car came to rest, upside down, against a tree at the bottom of the hill.

Silence settled on the countryside. Alex let go of the steering wheel, worked himself clear of the twisted metal, slid on his shoulders across the roof and out the gaping hole where the right door had been. He stood next to the car a moment in the cold night, then automatically lit a cigarette. "Holy Jesus," he said aloud.

Although I changed the name of it, the stretch of road I describe is a real one, and I had often driven it myself, trying to see how fast I could take it, but I'd never had a hot car under me, and I wasn't much of a driver, and of course I'd never driven it anywhere near as fast as Alex does. I doubt that anyone could drive it as fast as he does, and I doubt that anyone could walk away from a wreck like the one I have described. Yet I had walked away from a total wreck — I had been a passenger, not the driver — and we had left the road at an insanely high speed, but we had *not* rolled. Like Alex we had stood there afterward in the appalled silence, checking ourselves for damages, saying things like, "Holy Jesus."

## 3

I NEVER ONCE ALLUDE to Billy's death, but the shadow of it lies over the entire manuscript. Evan Carlyle, the character I used as a stand-in for myself, is saturated with pain and never able to figure out why. In *The Rest Is Silence* he isn't the budding Beat writer he was in my high school story — now he's a heartbroken loser with no goals or ambitions, so fucked up he can barely function, much like me at my worst in those days. He's surrounded by a fairly large cast of characters — the boys who hang out at Alex Warner's garage. They're propelled through the narrative by a great sluice of alcohol as overwhelming as the Ohio River at full flood. Things happen to them, and they do things, but there's not much of a plot. Evan spends the entire book brooding about his lost girlfriend, getting piss drunk, barfing, passing out, waking up hung over, and then doing it all over again.

If someone had commissioned me to describe the most unsavory aspects of American white boy culture in the late 1950s, I couldn't have done a better job. There's a nasty childish quality to these guys. The requirements for leadership are simple and well-known by anyone who has ever grown up white and male in small-town

Appalachia — the ability to remain upright after drinking prodigious amounts of alcohol, drive twisty mountain roads at insanely high speeds, beat the crap out of enemy combatants, and fuck anything that moves.

Meanwhile, a low-level homoerotic buzz is sounding. The boys joke constantly about masturbation — at one point Alex suggests that they turn out the lights and have a circle jerk — but god help anybody who might take this as anything more than a joke. The worst thing you can be is feminine — just before he beats the bejesus out of a boy from an enemy group, Alex calls him "honey" — and the worst thing you can call another boy is "faggot." Girls are worse than "other" — they're weird, distant, incomprehensible beings who are scarcely human. The boys talk about girls and women using exactly the same language that Henry Miller does.

Yet there's something else going on here too, something important and authentic about boys and cars and the time and the place. It's as though there's a whole other universe running parallel to the one where these fucked up boys live — one that is so painful and strange, so unbearably sweet and filled with such incompressible power that they will risk their lives merely to get a glimpse of it. The only way they know how to get there is by running the road.

> As the car rolls, the motion moves out, wheels
> out to night and rushing light, then the sorrow
> moves, moves under, and the current is too

strange to speak of. Behind the rushing car, the lights, the whipping air, the sound of the tires, is something strange, a deep current, a river. Sad now, but the power is vast potential, vast current, touching strange interconnections. Somewhere, very distant, the sound of a cigarette burning with a drag is a small grasshopper noise, disquieting.

Caught suddenly, a fractional miscalculation, the car fishtails out sideways to the road and rock piles sweep across the line of vision. Then lights line fast streaks across the windshield as the wheel sweeps over. The car rights itself, screaming, hits the next curve, makes it. Already the National Road, off to the left, is glowing like a fallen Milky Way.

ALTHOUGH I'VE OVERSTATED their stories to make them a bit larger than life, most of my characters resemble people I actually knew, doing the kinds of things we actually did, but two of them don't. The only girl in the book, Evan's lost love, is one of them. I'd been writing about her ever since I'd started jotting down stories in the eighth grade — she's the beautiful young ballet dancer with the terrible stage mom — so she'd already had a number of other names before she became "Linda" in this manuscript. She's little more than a pretty puppet for the author to move around at will.

The other alien character is David Warner. Alex never had a little brother before, and he never will again, but he has one now. Alex is a compact dark wiry guy with curly black hair and beer-colored eyes, yet, defying genetics, I've given him a younger brother who is six feet tall, blonde and blue-eyed, and so pretty-boy gorgeous that girls turn to stare at him on the street. David Warner defines himself as a game player—he's a pool shark, poker ace, and pinball wizard. He lives in his grandmother's attic, sleeps much of the day, stays up all night reading Modernist poetry, memorizing the chess games of the masters, or wandering the streets at dawn. He keeps this "reflective" side of himself secret and presents to the world as a buffoon, sometimes spouting a Shakespearean baby talk that generates sentences like, "Thinkst thee we shouldst?" He's like a character who has inexplicably dropped in from a silly British novel from the 1930s.

While I was writing *The Rest Is Silence*, I thought that Evan Carlyle was telling the story of Alex Warner much like Nick Carraway tells the story of Jay Gatsby, but that's not what I was actually doing. After the book gets going, the energy gradually shifts away from Alex until it becomes focused almost entirely on his younger brother.

Who the hell *is* this guy? Okay, let's look at what he actually does. One of Dave's primary functions in the narrative is to provide a running criticism of his brother. "Alex is just as you see him all the way to the bottom," he tells Linda. "People think he's deep, why he's not even shallow! He's like an onion. You can peel back the layers all you want to, but you still have onion clear to the bottom." Dave knows exactly why Alex wrecked his car — "If he hadn't made that run, his balls would have dropped off."

When Alex and Evan get monumentally drunk and barf all over the bathroom, Dave is the one who takes care of them. "Just call me Florence Nightingale," he says. Dave is the only one who will actually sit and *listen* to Evan's endless laments about his lost love. Dave is the only character who feels empathy for other people. He gives his pinball and poker winnings to Alex so he can buy a motorcycle to replace his wrecked car — because Alex without wheels is not Alex. When Evan breaks down and cries in an alley, Dave is the one who comforts him. When Evan tries to apologize, Dave says, "Shut up. Just cry."

In a key scene Linda arrives out of nowhere to get into bed with Dave. There's nothing in the plot that would justify her doing that; she does it for no other reason than the author wanted her to. They talk for a while, and then she kisses him.

Dave's mind was derailed, ran in a rapid circle
to orient itself. He realized that he had been
completely unaware for the past two hours
that there had been a girl in his bed. He had
forgotten, or never remembered, that this was
a stock situation, a stock symbol, and that
he should have reacted in a certain specific
manner. He had not felt even slightly aroused.
"Don't be in such a hurry," he said.

Reading this scene now my first thought is, oh my god, he's gay. Well, no, maybe not — maybe *proto*-gay. But no, that's not right either. What was I doing? I must have still been fighting my inner war of opposites. On the one side there's the *truly masculine* Alex Warner, and on the other?

David Warner is the latest incarnation of the feminine boys who had been appearing in my stories since I'd begun writing them. We're told that as a child, he had often been mistaken for a girl, and now, in adolescence, he's as beautiful as I had wanted to be in my pink shirt period. His bemused visitor-from-another-planet position is one that I had often occupied myself, and I too had read modernist poetry all night long and walked the streets at dawn. He's *like a girl* — some version of myself, not as I was but as I wanted to be — and then that *other* version of myself, Evan Carlyle, is me as the hopeless drunk trying his best to be *a real boy* and knowing he'll never make it.

### 4

HALFWAY THROUGH *The Rest Is Silence* the eldest of the Warner boys drops into the plot — sadistic big brother Bob who terrorized Alex and Dave when they were children. If Alex is *truly masculine*, then Robert Warner is even more masculine — absolutely one-hundred-percent dipshit zero-brains male. He eats, sleeps, fights, and fucks, and that's all he does. He's in the Marines, and he's spoiling for a fight.

To give our team some enemies, I introduce a pack of Canden High boys — rich kids from "out the pike." They think they're tough, but of course they lose the first round to Alex and Bob and retreat to their cars. This sets my characters in motion, chasing each other around the Ohio Valley in the late August heat wave, in a stagnant stifling night punctuated by the heat lightning that, as I was writing it, I saw as Faulknerian.

Alex and Bob eventually catch up to the Canden High boys and deliver retribution complete with broken bones and kicked out teeth, then go off to engage each other in an all-night drinking contest. The heat wave finally breaks, and a cleansing thunderstorm rolls into the valley. Because I was steeped in Joyce, I wanted to give my main character an epiphany. Evan had to learn something, didn't he? Otherwise, what was the point of all these pages?

> Something about Linda, some clue, trace of forgotten meaning. Bright small flame of a girl. He could not control the movement of his mind, only darted along behind it, picking up the pieces. Whatever the movement touched, reality splintered into a thousand fiery fragments. It was not Linda. *She had nothing to do with it. She had only been a carrier of some vital living thing, a reflection of beauty.*

I haven't added the italics; they're in the original. So what was the vital living thing Linda had been carrying? What was the beauty she had been reflecting?

At the end of the book Robert Warner is knifed to death in a barroom brawl. This happens offstage, when Bob is back on base. The boys have been scattered in various directions, but the entire cast reunites in my fictitious town of Harrod for the funeral. They retire to a local bar, get pissed, and then gradually begin to trickle away. "The rest is silence," David Warner says and walks out of the bar — and out of the novel — and out of the author's narrative forever.

As the novel ends, only Evan and Alex are left. "What do we do now?" Evan asks. "Beats the shit out of me," Alex says.

It's been over fifty years since I wrote this stuff, and if I don't have some distance from it by now, I'm not going to be getting any. The boys in *The Rest Is Silence* are curiously ungrounded in anything like a real world. An adult who read the manuscript shortly after I finished it said, "They have no parents!" She was absolutely right, and they have no jobs either. Alex is the only one who seems to work at anything, but what exactly? He lives at the garage, sells people gas, works on their cars, but seems to have no boss. Evan is too fucked up to work at anything, so who's supporting him? Dave is still in high school and lives with his grandmother, but we never meet her, and we don't hear a word about high school. The Polish guys who hang around might work at something, but if they do, we never hear about it. The story is emphatically set in West Virginia, but we're told nothing of what it might mean to be set there. To me, the author, the book seems closer to my vehement high school essays than a work of fiction. I was interested in *boys*. I was exploring various versions of masculinity.

The *truly masculine* Alex Warner is my somewhat idealized version of the good old mountain boy. The ugly dipshit Robert Warner is an exemplar of the kind of over-the-top masculinity that we would now call toxic. Drunken Evan Carlyle reproduces the useless drone masculinity of my pathetic uncle Bill. The *vital living thing* that Linda is carrying is the one thing that these boys most intensely desire — that their author most intensely desired — the one thing that they also most intensely fear and despise — the feminine. But David Warner is different; he's the only kind and decent person in the story. It's no accident that he's Alex Warner's little brother — that he's blonde and blue-eyed like my dead almost little brother. It's also no accident that he gets Hamlet's last line.

"Working through some shit" is a technical term employed by creative writing instructors when confronted with a student manuscript in which they see lots of interesting things that the author is unaware of. It would take me years to work through this shit.

EXCEPT FOR THE REFERENCE to Lonnie Donegan's 1959 hit, "Does Your Chewing Gum Lose Its Flavor?" there is nothing in *The Rest Is Silence* to nail it down in time, but it is looking firmly backward into the 1950s. There's not a single reference to Vietnam or the draft — even though every male character in it would have been draft eligible and I would have been acutely aware of that because I suffered through my US Army physical right in the middle of writing it, literally putting the manuscript down to go to the exam and picking it up again when I came back.

I had come to my own conclusions about Vietnam by then. I was a reader of *The Catholic Worker*, an admirer of the American Friends Service Committee, and a member of the Student Peace Union. When I'd been at WVU, I'd checked out a dozen or so books from the university library and spent a few days reading them. The main thing the Vietnamese wanted was to be left alone; they had been fighting a colonial war against the French, and we had inherited it. The Vietnamese had always been hereditary enemies of the Chinese so there was no way that they were going to allow their country to be turned into a puppet state of China. If we simply ended the war and went home, Vietnam was likely to turn into a relatively benign little communist country something like Yugoslavia, no threat to American interests whatsoever. Then why were we in Vietnam? It didn't make any sense — but then a lot of American history didn't make any sense.

When I filled out the forms for my army physical, I claimed to have every disease or disorder mentioned, from yellow fever to wetting the bed. Years later, when I would first hear Arlo Guthrie's "Alice's Restaurant," I wouldn't be able to stop laughing because my experience had been so similar. I don't know if where I was sent was called "the Group W Bench" as it is in Arlo's account, but it was indeed a bench and a long one. Sitting on it were the fuck-ups of the day, young males of various shapes and sizes wearing nothing but our shoes and underwear, all of us waiting to see an army doctor. The one who interviewed me could have stepped directly out of a cartoon — a bald fat middle-aged man smoking the remains of a cigar as thick as a banana. He looked over my file. It seemed to amuse him that I had checked every box, but there was only one box that counted. He asked me if I'd ever had sex with a boy.

Everybody back in those days thought that all feminine boys were automatically gay. It was something you didn't have to talk about because everybody "knew" it was true, so of course I'd wondered if I was gay. Because my sexual interest was focused so intensely on girls, it didn't seem likely, but I was attracted to the occasional boy so maybe I was kidding myself — *repressing* something, as I'd learned to say from the Freudians. Eventually, when I had the opportunity to check it out for myself, I took advantage of it. Afterward I knew that

I was still primarily attracted to girls, but having sex with a boy had been an entirely positive experience for me — friendly, warm, physically satisfying, and fun — so positive that it had left me with the conviction that any culture that forbids such things is sick to its core. Yes, I told the doctor, I'd had sex with a boy.

"Okay, son," he said, "and what do you want to do with your life?"

"I want to be a writer."

"Do you want to write comedy or tragedy?"

"Tragedy."

"An *American* tragedy? Who wrote that?"

"Theodore Dreiser."

"That's right! Do you want to be in the army?"

"No."

"Well, you're not going to be." He stamped my form 4-F, unfit to serve, and I was no longer draft eligible. That should have been a relief, and I suppose it was. So what *was* I going to do with the rest of my life? The line that I had given Alex at the end of *The Rest Is Silence* had by then become my personal motto — "Beats the shit out of me."

**6**

FOR YEARS I had a recurring nightmare that I had committed some unspeakable crime and any minute was going to be arrested for it and sent to prison for the rest of my life. There is plenty of evidence against me — a body buried under the floorboards. While I was having these nightmares — sometimes as often as several times a week — I could never figure out why I was guilty. Now I would say that it was obvious — I was alive and Billy wasn't.

I didn't decide to make my home in Boston; that's where I ran out of forward motion. I'd been on the road so long that every highway was beginning to look like every other highway. I was tired of standing around in Howard Johnson parking lots with my thumb out, tired of spending my nights in piss-ass Greyhound terminals waiting for an 8:00 a.m. bus. Tired? Hell, I was as beat as any character out of Kerouac. I wanted to stay somewhere for a while. Even though my own student days were long over, I liked being around Harvard, liked walking around the Square with the Harvard boys and the Radcliffe girls, liked wandering through the library — one of the truly great ones. I seemed to be able to find work whenever I really wanted it, and I worked at a number of odd jobs — some of them very odd. Whenever I was dead broke, I could always count on my mother for a few bucks. I can't remember how I did it, but somehow I got the attention of a literary agent. In my memory he's drunk most of the time, but that was okay, so was I. Here's what I remember him saying when he rejected my manuscript: "Although there is some good writing — even some great writing — in this novel, I do not believe it would be a commercial success, concerned as it is with an almost mindless violence."

I was reading Hammett, Chandler, and Ross Macdonald, and rereading them to see how they did it, so I wrote a hard-boiled murder mystery. It had some gender switching and lots more mindless violence. The agent took that one and sent it out, and there were some encouraging rejections but no takers. I was still trying to think of myself as a writer — *The Rest Is Silence* was my proof — but I was following in the footsteps of my uncle Bill, a man I had always despised. I'd get loaded and read my manuscript over yet again and stuff it with even more notes outlining possible future rewrites, but the drinking had become more important than the notes.

Meanwhile, out in the real world, Lyndon Johnson was bombing the shit out of North Vietnam. We had five hundred thousand troops over there, and the draft was going full tilt, taking anyone who could walk upright. Smart white boys could still get out of it by getting married or staying in school, but black boys and poor white boys were being drafted by the thousands and fed into the meat grinder. Guys who'd been in the war early were starting to come back thoroughly fucked up, and I'd met some of them. "Obscene" was the word often used by people opposed to the war, and I thought it was the right word.

One afternoon I stopped in the Harvard Square liquor store to get my supply for the night. When I was low on my luck, I drank port wine because that gave you the most bang for your buck, but I had a few extra dollars so I bought cheap bourbon. Out on the street I passed a street vender selling an underground newspaper. He had the most hair I had ever seen on a male, not only a huge tangled mop on top but a full beard and mustache. I gave him a few coins and took a copy of his paper. When I got home, I read it. We had to stop the war — that was the central message of it — and I wholeheartedly agreed. I drank steadily and read that paper over and over. Just before I passed out, I had an insight. It was a fairly simple insight; if it hadn't been, I couldn't have had it. It was obvious by now that I was utterly useless to myself, but maybe I could be useful *to other people.* This is an extremely powerful psychological move, and I recommend it to anyone who thinks that they're at the end of their rope.

Nobody stops drinking simply by deciding to and then doing it, but I didn't know that. I woke up the next morning, poured what was left of the fifth down the sink, and quit. It would be nearly three years before I had a drink again. I went out into the world, gulped my standard hangover cure — a "frappe," which is what people in Boston call a milkshake — and made my way to the rat-hole office of that underground newspaper. It was full of hairy people. "You said you need writers," I told them. "I'm a writer." In those days the Movement would take all of the time you had to give it, and I gave it all of mine.

# part VII

# THE MOVEMENT

## 1

I'VE ALREADY WRITTEN a fictionalized account of the end of the 1960s in a big fat novel called *Looking Good*, and I don't see any point in doing that work all over again from another angle, so I'm going to try to stay focused here and finish what I started — a memoir about writing and gender — but I have to take us on a few sidetracks first.

I can't find an online reference to this particular event, so what I'm about to write is purely from memory, and I might have got some of it wrong. It was probably in 1969. I can't remember the exact location, although it was in a church in Cambridge or Boston. Noam Chomsky was debating some dude from, the best I can recall, the

Rand Corporation. The church was packed. The Rand guy went first. He presented the standard-issue US government argument for the Vietnam War. He was used to addressing crowds. He gave a glib, polished, and entertaining speech.

Chomsky was not a good speaker. He was a university professor, and that's exactly what he sounded like — flat, dry, uninflected and unimpressed. He quoted from a massive amount of material, all of it from memory, citing his sources, complete with page numbers, to argue that the United States had no business in Vietnam whatsoever. He rolled over the Rand guy and squashed him flat. Then, when he was finished, Chomsky looked out at the people in the church — that was *us*, the dissident white kids — the New Left, or hip left, or counter culture left, or whatever label you might want to put on us.

I've just done a Google search to remind myself of what we actually looked like. Images of "student protest Vietnam" reveal that my memory has made us hairier than we actually were; some of us had a lot of hair, but others of us were still in the process of growing it. In the early days of the Movement some of the women would have been wearing miniskirts, but after Women's Liberation hit town, they would have stopped doing that, and by the end of the '60s most of us in the Boston political scene, no matter our gender, would have been wearing jeans, boots, and men's work shirts — a youth uniform that's still around, although its cultural significance has shifted. I don't have a picture of myself from that time, but I'd grown enough hair that people told me I looked like the young Benjamin Franklin.

I was living on the margins, holed up in a series of rat-trap apartments, crashing with other people, and for a while lived in an anarchist commune. I had no regular income, but if you were a middle-class white kid in the '60s, money wasn't that hard to get, and whenever any of us had "the coin," as we called it, we helped each other out. I hardly ever had to pay for weed — it was just around — and whenever I was absolutely tapped out, I could always get a gig as a typist for a temp agency. I was writing for what we called "the underground press," which, of course, paid nothing, but I considered that my full-time job. Later on we would be remembered as "the new journalists," or, more colorfully, "gonzo journalists." We considered objectivity to be an illusion, a capitalist sham, and we were unabashedly partisan. *They* had their media, and *we* had ours; they frequently lied — remember MacNamara? — but we were committed to telling the truth, as elusive as that truth might sometimes be.

The Constitution of the United States protected free speech — except when it didn't. The Boston Five had been convicted for what they had said and written because, as the government claimed, they had been "encouraging resistance" to the Selective Service Act. Noam Chomsky and his allies had given us their take on what the government was up to: "It is impossible to conduct a brutal war of aggression in the name of an enlightened and informed citizenry; either the war must be terminated, or democratic rights, including the right to information and free discussion, must be restricted." The original indictment brought against the Boston Five also mentioned "diverse other persons, some known and others unknown." That included me. I'm not claiming any special status for myself; the underground press movement involved thousands of people.

At one time or another all of us must have felt a sense of utter futility; I know that I did — as though I were spending every minute of my worrisome life running at a dead sprint to arrive absolutely nowhere. Chomsky looked out at us — this collection of New Left freaks who had crammed the church that night — and said, "You're the only thing keeping the United States government from doing what it wants to in Southeast Asia. Whatever you're doing, keep on doing it."

I felt blessed.

WHEN WE TALKED ABOUT "the Movement," we meant something larger than merely the anti-war movement; we supported all liberation struggles. In our chunk of the Movement, the white New Left, you could find damned near any leftist point of view you could imagine — from old-time Marxists, Leninists, and Trotskyites, through a wide array of anarchists, including Abbie Hoffman's capricious Yippies, to the Age of Aquarius kids who believed in love. Of course we considered ourselves allied to the Black Power Movement, but by the time that

I entered the scene in 1968, the Black left and the white left were to all intents and purposes entirely separate.

Much has been written about the evolution of the Black Power Movement and that's not my story to tell except in the briefest of summaries. The Freedom Summer project in 1964 appeared to have been a crucial turning point. The wonderfully named Council of Federated Organizations (COFO) brought hundreds of northern volunteers, most of them white kids from affluent families, into Mississippi to help register Black voters and to conduct freedom schools. Mississippi was widely considered to be the absolute heart of "the Southern way of life," and the state lived up to its reputation; the arrival of the volunteers set off multiple arrests, beatings, bombings, and burnings that continued all summer.

Some of the COFO organizers had argued that the presence of white kids might draw more media attention to the plight of Black folks in Mississippi, and they proved to be right. Three civil rights workers, two white and one Black, vanished. It seemed likely that they had been lynched, and vanishing *white kids* did bring massive media attention — *New York Times* headlines. With considerable reluctance, the FBI came to look for them; then the US Navy joined the search. In August their bodies were found hidden under a dam.

Some of the organizers of Freedom Summer were deeply troubled about using white kids as a fulcrum — appealing to America's racism — and they began to see the need for an all-Black movement. By 1967 that line of thought had evolved to the point that the Student Nonviolent Coordinating Committee (SNCC) asked their white staff to resign, suggesting that they organize in their own community — and that is exactly what they did. White kids who had begun their work in the Civil Rights Movement often became key players in the anti-war movement. When I became active, I met several of the Freedom Summer volunteers and heard their stories of the unrelenting heat of Mississippi — of jeering white folks, menacing cops, and that sick sense of dread down deep in the belly that never goes away.

"CONSENSUS POLITICS" — talking things over until you all pretty much agree — was one of the things we had learned from the Civil Rights Movement. My experience tells me that it only works for small groups of people who live together. Large groups looking for consensus were often so bogged down in endless meetings that they couldn't accomplish anything or ended up being run by a small unelected subgroup who made all the decisions while everyone else simply went along with them. Those in my particular group — mostly underground press types — weren't actually living together, but we spent so much time together that we might as well have been. We loved to talk, and consensus politics worked for us just fine.

Some of my friends refused political labels, but many of us identified as anarchists, often with something added to specify what kind — emulating not the scary bomb-throwing boys but theorists like Bakunin or Kropotkin who argued that we don't need a state to govern us. We wanted more than merely an end to the Vietnam war; we wanted to utterly transform society. Like Chomsky, one of my heroes, I called myself an "anarcho-syndicalist."

"Politically correct" is now a term used almost exclusively by conservatives when they want to hurl an insult at someone — usually a young person — anywhere left of center, but it was originally *our* term, and *it was a joke*. We would have been arguing for a while, and then someone would say, "Okay, comrades, is that the *correct line*?" and we'd all smile because it was so ridiculous. It was Lenin who used the word "correct," but we were not Leninists, and we didn't believe in central committees, vanguard parties, or any *correct line*. We believed in participatory democracy, direct action, and building the new society in the shell of the old. We admired some things about the Cuban Revolution and criticized others. We didn't much care for the Soviet Union or — after initial misguided enthusiasm — Mao's China. We didn't trust Leninists of any stripe and quoted Rosa Luxemburg to them: "The mistakes that are made by a truly revolutionary workers' movement are immeasurably more fruitful and more valuable than the infallibility of the best possible 'Central Committee.'"

AS A MEMBER OF the underground press, I attended all Movement events within driving distance — protests, sit-ins, public debates, sanctuaries — and if I remember the high-kick adrenaline rush of walking into the "liberated zone" of an occupied building as emblematic of the time, just as emblematic is my memory of myself alone in a small dingy room somewhere, stretched out on a narrow bed with an old table lamp at my shoulder, reading furiously, giving myself a crash course in political theory. Beginning with the realization that our government was lying to us, had been lying to us for years, we moved on to consider the possibility that *anybody* might be lying. Suspicious and skeptical, we felt as though we had to re-create all human knowledge from the ground up, a fairly big order for kids in their twenties.

I wrote for a number of underground newspapers. I first offered my services to the *Journal of the New England Resistance*. They argued for individual moral witness against the war — suggesting that draft-eligible young men burn their draft cards and do the jail time if they had to. I admired their position for its purity, but I also saw it as hopelessly naïve and thought that I would be far more useful out of jail rather than in it, so I never burned my draft card and was never officially a member of the Resistance. Those of us who gradually came together around the notion of publishing an underground paper had a much more rough and ready approach to politics — anything that works. We wanted to make things so difficult for the government to conduct the Vietnam War that they would stop doing it; we also wanted to get at the root causes that had made the war possible.

Over the next two years we published several papers. First we were *The Boston Free Press*, but then when it was pointed out to us is that there was already a paper of that name, we became *The Free Press of Boston*, and finally we merged with *Broadside* to become *Broadside and the Free Press*. I was also hired by Boston college radio station WBUR to produce an hour-long show once a week called "The Underground News," and they actually paid me to do it. The great thing about writing for the underground press was that I could say anything I damned well pleased.

## 2

MY BIBLE IN THOSE DAYS was Gary Snyder's *Earth House Hold*. I read it so many times that I practically memorized it, and I wanted everyone else to read it too, so I kept giving away my copies and buying new ones. I loved how personal Snyder's writing was — much of it based on journal entries — and I also loved how concise he could be, getting right to the heart of things. For me the essay entitled "Buddhism and the Coming Revolution" was the heart of the heart. "The mercy of the West has been social revolution; the mercy of the East has been individual insight into the basic self/void. We need both."

I loved Snyder's concern for all life on the planet. To counter the Christian notion that man has dominion over nature, he offered the view held by many other cultures that we are not separate from nature, certainly not superior to it, but part of it — as the Chinese sages had said, we are merely one of the ten thousand things that arise, manifest, and vanish. Snyder made my politics as much Buddhist as it was anarchist.

My cousin's death had chopped my life in half, and I'd been afraid that I'd lost a hopeful earlier version of myself, but reading Snyder connected me back to reading *The Dharma Bums* when I'd been sixteen — "You can't fall off a mountain!" — connected me back to the boy who had created Butch Carlyle, the Supergirl who was "sad and lonely and melancholy and beat" and on her way to becoming a future Buddha. I had walked the streets of Wheeling and read everything as a clue; now I was walking the streets of Cambridge and Boston, looking for clues again, picking up the dropped threads of my earlier life, and Snyder was the catalyst. He fit perfectly into our politics. Here he is at his most concise: "The state is legalized greed."

### 3

AS THE CLIMACTIC and optimistic year 1968 segued into scary 1969, many Movement women were being swept up into what we now call "Second Wave Feminism," although no one used that term at the time — we said "Women's Liberation." With the exception of Simone de Beauvoir's *The Second Sex* and Betty Friedan's *The Feminine Mystique*, the books that we consider to be classics of the Second Wave hadn't been written yet, and

it was very much a do-it-yourself period in the movement — young women making up feminist theory on
their own, coming up with new ideas every day — and
the huge energy of that creative period was readily appar-
ent even to men like me who were watching from the
sidelines. Several of the women in our commune were
members of the socialist women's collective Bread and
Roses. They would come back from collective meetings
glowing with excitement. They were onto something
vitally important, and they knew it.

Another significant women's group in Boston was
Cell 16 who deftly avoided the term "women" by advo-
cating for *female* liberation. They sponsored a showing
of *The Queen*, a documentary film about a drag beauty
contest, offered free admission to any man who would
show up in drag, but I don't recall that anyone took them
up on it. Even though we in the audience were watching while the contestants went through the elaborate
processes necessary to transform themselves, it was difficult not to read them as women by the time they were
finished — and that was exactly the point. "One is not
born, but rather becomes a woman," Beauvoir wrote,
and if Cell 16 wanted to demonstrate just how much
that becoming depends upon constructed image, they
couldn't have found a better way to do it.

ANYTHING THAT CAUGHT ON was circulated through the
women's friendship circles lickety-split. For a time, every
woman I knew had either just finished reading, or was

about to read, Virginia Woolf's *A Room of One's Own*, so of course I read it too. Woolf's notion of androgyny has been criticized by a series of theorists who seem willfully determined to miss her point. Here's what she actually said:

> And I went on amateurishly to sketch a plan of the soul so that in each of us two powers preside, one male, one female; and in the man's brain the man predominates over the woman, and in the woman's brain the woman predominates over the man. The normal and comfortable state of being is that when the two live in harmony together, spiritually co-operating. If one is a man, still the woman part of his brain must have effect; and a woman also must have intercourse with the man in her. Coleridge perhaps meant this when he said that a great mind is androgynous. It is when this fusion takes place that the mind is fully fertilised and uses all its faculties.

None of us would have taken Woolf's use of the word "brain" as an argument for biological essentialism. We were stoners, and we would have translated "brain" into "mind" — another matter altogether. She was talking about consciousness, and so were we. From R.D. Laing we had learned about the politics of *experience*, and if you have lived all of your life on one side or the other of the pink and blue divide, that experience has determined your consciousness. What Woolf was recommending to writers was a profound empathy for those on the other side. It occurred to me that if my consciousness wasn't androgynous, then nobody's was.

I told my story — roughly the same one I'm telling here — to a close friend in the Movement. I'd told parts of it before, but I'd never told all of it before. "You were girl-identified," she told me. "That's not a bad thing. That's a good thing."

We agreed that revolutionary consciousness had to be androgynous. For the first time in my life it occurred to me that there might be nothing wrong with me.

IN THE APRIL 1969 ISSUE of *The Free Press* I wrote a long article titled "Sexual Liberation: Androgyny?" Repetitive, meandering, frequently lost in sidebar details, riddled with as many citations as a university paper, easily twice the length it should have been, it's far from my best writing from that time, but it's a good sample of what I'd been thinking.

Riffing off Engels, I open with speculation on how women became oppressed in the first place, and then I wander around commenting on everything from restrictive Victorian fashion to high-school dress codes. I cite folks who thought that the distinctions between the sexes were dissolving, attack some psychiatrist who claimed that alcohol fits nicely into our culture because it fosters masculine behavior whereas marijuana makes us feminine, note the arrival of androgyny in the fashion world, and consider McLuhan's notion that the mini-skirt is a "cool" image. Whenever I want to make a really heavy point, I quote Simone de Beauvoir. Despite my title, I don't mention Virginia Woolf or Coleridge, and I don't discuss androgyny at all. The main purpose of my article — and I return to it again and again — is to advocate for the nascent Woman's Liberation movement. I begin at the outset by saying that I'm addressing "the male oppressor class," so when I say "we," I mean men.

> We need Women's Liberation because the thrust for change must come from the oppressed class. Unless we are pushed, we will not change; we have too much invested interest in the status quo. We need Women's Liberation to make us acutely uncomfortable, to shake us, to push us out of our ruts. If we can get our heads together and groove behind the trip, Women's Liberation will help us to liberate ourselves.

Near the end, I ask a series of questions. I would recommend that contemporary readers make the effort to imagine themselves so far back in time that these questions would seem fresh, surprising, or even alarming — as they did in 1969.

> What is so goddamned sacrosanct about the family unit; why should children be considered the property of their parents (or, for that matter,

anybody's property); why should a wife take her husband's last name; why should our first names always indicate our sex; why should certain articles of clothing be taboo for individuals because of their sex; why should men have little constellations of female satellites around them to do their shit work, and why should men feel demeaned if their fingers ever touch a typewriter key (I'm not talking about just the business world, look in any Movement office); why are "normal" men threatened to the point of rage by homosexuals, lesbians, and other "deviants"; why is it impossible for us to love each other simply as human beings?

Halfway through the article a lifetime of bottled up rage spills out of me and onto the page.

When our phony self-image of masculinity is brought into question by women, we often react by calling these women "castrative," forgetting that this kind of symbolic castration is something in our own heads, not in the world. And, if the presence of balls is defined by a willingness to fight at the drop of a hat over the most trivial matters, a readiness to screw anything that walks, a compulsion to defend our "masculinity" by fighting in a war we might suspect is wrong and stupid, a dedication to

exploiting and using women as things so we can
have something to brag about in the bar with
the boys, then our "castration" is something
that is long overdue.

Despite the tone of fuck-you bravado I'd adopted
for this piece, the main thing I'd been feeling when I'd
been writing it had been a gut-wrenching anxiety. I could
sense that I was entering dangerous territory. I'd leaned
so heavily on Simone de Beauvoir and other writers
because I'd wanted all the allies I could get.

It was reported back to me through the underground
whisper network that male heavies in the Movement
were not grooving on the trip. "Who the hell is this
guy?" they were asking about me. From their point
of view Women's Lib was pulling energy out of the
Movement — it was certainly pulling *women* out of the
Movement — shifting the focus from serious things like
the war and third-world liberation movements to trivial
things like — well, like what? Women talking to each
other?

### 4

I REMEMBER NOW several incidents that signaled the
end of the road to me. I became friends with a fellow
anarchist who was visiting Boston. She was heavy into
"the ecology movement," as we called it then, and I
decided to devote one of my radio shows to it and asked

her to help me. As we began working on the project, it became clear that she knew a lot more about ecology than I did, so we switched roles — I turned the show over to her and gave her technical assistance. That carbon emissions were playing a large part in destroying the planet had not yet become clear, but she had plenty of other examples of how we were creating a world that might one day be best suited for cockroaches. We blended spoken word with music and produced a show that was, I thought, both a beautifully composed soundscape and a call for action that was just as alarming as it should be.

Not long after we aired our show, one of the local FM stations was devoting a week to ecology. I dropped off a tape of our show, suggested that it might fit into their programming. I didn't hear anything back from them, but I can be a persistent son of a bitch when I have to, and I bugged them until I got an appointment with their top DJ. By then, their ecology week was long over. The DJ slapped our tape onto a deck and we listened to the opening. "Wow," he said, "she's really good. She's blended her music just the way we do it."

"Well," I said, "you could have aired it." What I didn't say was, "If you had bothered to listen to it."

He took my meaning, apologized. He simply hadn't gotten around to it. So much heavy shit, you know, so much shit coming down. "We've been deluged, man. You dig?"

I suggested that he might want to interview my friend. There was an idea, he said. He might consider doing that. Then he asked me, "Is she revolutionary?"

I was so stunned by his question I couldn't find any way to answer it. What he was doing might be called "alternative," but it was fueled by the American music industry and that meant the big bucks. You tuned into his station if you wanted to check out the latest LP by the Beatles or Dylan or the Stones, if you wanted to hear the likes of Creedence Clearwater Revival, the Band, or the Jefferson Airplane, if you wanted to be introduced to brand new artists working in that art form called "rock," that art form we considered to be *ours*. My little one-hour program on college radio had a few hundred listeners if I was lucky; his station had thousands.

You colossal smooth-ass arrogant prick, I thought, how can you sit there with your razor-cut hair and designer bell-bottoms in your gleaming state-of-the-art studio and have the unmitigated fucking gall to ask me with a straight face, "IS SHE REVOLUTIONARY?" He was selling revolution. I had never understood more fully what the Marxists meant by "commodity fetishism" — how capitalism can absorb damned near anything and sell it back to us.

I WAS NOT A MEMBER of SDS (Students for a Democratic Society), and neither were any of my closest friends and allies in the Movement, but we watched from a distance as SDS disintegrated into warring factions and

destroyed itself. The most loud-mouthed and belliger-
ent of those factions called itself "Weatherman" after the
line in the Dylan song, "You don't need a weatherman to
know which way the wind blows." They idealized third-
world liberation movements, romanticized violence, and
seemed to me utterly ignorant of the historical context
of anything. By the fall of '69 they were planning an
action for October in Chicago — The Days of Rage. All
of us were supposed to converge on Chicago and bring
the war home. We were supposed to take to the streets
and fuck things up. On posters and propaganda leaflets,
they featured the word "Wargasm."

There was an unwritten rule in the Movement
that you don't criticize your allies in public, but it had
occurred to me that the Weather people were not allies —
in fact, they were beginning to look remarkably like
enemies — so I went after them in *The Free Press*. I translated their call to action as "bring your balls to Chicago."
I lost friends over that article. Some Movement people
wouldn't even speak to me after that.

Somewhat later I got a call from a woman activist
from Bread and Roses, someone I had never met. She
asked if I would like to have coffee with her. I had no
idea what she wanted, but it turned out that she too had
criticized Weatherman, had done what the Situationists
called a *détournement* on them — that's when you take
someone's propaganda and alter it in such a way that it
becomes yours. She and many of the women in Bread and
Roses had been profoundly offended by the Wargasm

poster that had equated sex with violence, so she had written critical comments all over it and republished it. Word had come back to her from people she trusted saying that Weatherman had been really pissed off at my article and her criticism. "We're on their hit list," she said.

What hit list? I'd never heard about any hit list. "The list of people who are to be shot after the revolution," she said.

We rapped for a while, concluded that there was not a whole hell of a lot we could do about it. "I just thought you should know," she told me. Neither of us believed that the kind of violent revolution Weatherman advocated was even remotely possible. Still, it was fairly creepy to imagine that there were people in town who wanted to kill us.

OKAY, so there was this guy, let's call him Karl. Many of the male Movement heavies were huge pricks, but he wasn't. Like me, he was a syndicalist, and he knew everything there was to know about the history of Marxism with a particular focus on the Spartacist movement. He was a friendly helpful guy without a speck of arrogance in him, his Marxism calm, reasonable, and definitely in for the long haul, and that seemed pretty good in the terrible year of 1970. The Movement was being hammered both by our enemies — the FBI, CIA, local cops, and other shadowy forces — and our "friends" like the barking-mad Weatherman faction that had morphed into the Weather Underground and in March had blown three of themselves up while making anti-personnel bombs. I want to emphasize this — they had been taping roofing nails to dynamite to make bombs designed *to kill people*. Those of us who still considered ourselves part of the Movement badly needed a calm stable center so we could move on into the future in a positive way. Some people in Boston, including me, were beginning to think that Karl might be near that stable center. When I say "people," I mean men. Women were dropping out of the Movement at a great rate, joining Women's Lib, leaving the men startled and stranded with nowhere to go.

One night Karl invited a number of us over to his place for dinner. By "us" I mean men. We went there to engage with that venerable Marxist question: "What is to be done, comrades?" The best I can remember, Karl was still in grad school, working on his PhD at Harvard, but I might have got that wrong. He had a nice student apartment, clean and orderly, one of those places that's crammed with books floor to ceiling, and he had an honest-to-god real desk — I remember that desk clearly — dark old wood, stacked high with impressive papers. He also had a girlfriend who was the only woman there. She was wearing a baby pink pantsuit.

I want to be sure that contemporary readers get the full impact of the baby pink pantsuit. This is too simple, but in the Women's Lib movement something like this formulation was at work — everything we call *feminine* had been imposed on girls and women by the male oppressor class while those bastards had kept all the good stuff, everything we call *masculine*, for themselves. *Feminine*, therefore, was bad and *masculine* was good, so Movement women, the serious ones, dressed exactly like their boyfriends, and their boyfriends were dressing exactly like *workers*. In 1970 no serious Movement woman in Boston would have worn a baby pink pantsuit under pain of death, but there she was in a baby pink pantsuit. The men settled in the living room to have a few beers, blow a little smoke, and rap about serious heavy shit. The girlfriend was alone in the kitchen, cooking dinner.

In response to the threat of Women's Lib, a Leninist motto had been floating around in Movement circles — "The woman question vanishes in practice." I could see immediately that it had not vanished in Karl's practice, and I was no longer interested in what he had to say about Rosa Luxemburg. I joined the girlfriend in the kitchen. It would have been impolite of me to mention her baby pink pantsuit, so I didn't. We liked each other immediately. We talked about cooking. She showed me how easy it is to remove the papery skin from a clove of garlic — using the flat side of a cooking knife, you simply squash it on a cutting board and it peels right off. No one had ever shown me how to do that before. We made coq au vin. It was delicious. To this day I follow the recipe she taught me.

NEAR THE END of my time in Boston I had a dream so powerful that it felt like a visitation. Gary Snyder walked into my bedroom, looked down at me where I was sleeping, and said, "You missed something in my book."

Later I would not remember what he looked like; he was simply a presence. I sat up in bed. "I've read your book over and over again," I said. "I don't think I missed anything."

"Yes, you did," he said, "and it's really important for you." He opened his book and pointed at the passage.

I woke up. My first thought was that I wouldn't find any passage like that. I was sure that the message for me must have been a dream message, so if I hadn't read it in the dream, it was lost forever. I found my copy of *Earth House Hold*, flipped through it quickly, and by God, there was the passage. Of course I had read it, but I'd completely missed the significance of it.

Comes a time when the poet must choose:
either to step deep in the stream of his people,
history, tradition, folding and folding himself
in wealth of persons and pasts; philosophy,
humanity, to become richly foundationed and
great and sane and ordered. Or, to step beyond
the bound onto the way out, into horrors and
angels, possible madness or silly Faustian
doom, possible utter transcendence, possible
enlightened return, possible ignominious
wormish perishing.

I'd been stepping beyond the bound for years, and I had indeed come terribly close to ignominious wormish perishing. There was no doubt which path I had to take now. I repeated "richly foundationed and great and sane and ordered" like a mantra.

## 5

BY 1970 the New Left was well on its way to disintegrating entirely, and I thought that perhaps the only good thing that might survive and grow into the future was the women's movement. The issues that my women friends were discussing in their consciousness-raising groups were exactly the kinds of things I'd been thinking about my entire life, and Women's Lib was pretty much the only political movement that still interested me. "We appreciate your support," a woman friend told me kindly, "but stop trying to be involved with us. This is something we have to do for ourselves. Go organize in your own community."

It made perfect sense to me that women had to do it for themselves, but as to organizing in *my own community*, that was another matter. I knew that I wasn't a straight man, and I wasn't a gay man either. I didn't know what my own community was.

After Nixon's incursions into Cambodia and the murder of students at Kent State, it looked as though the US was going to be involved in Southeast Asia forever and there was absolutely nothing any of us could do about it. I was burnt out and filled with despair. Paranoid about the possibility of my phone being tapped, I called my mother from a phone booth. "It looks like the revolution isn't going to happen any time soon," I told her. "I'm thinking of going to Canada." However odd that message might have sounded to her, she said what she'd always said, "Honey, you've got to do what you think's best." Looking back now, I can't imagine having a more supportive mother. She was always my number one fan, and anything I felt that I needed to do — however wacky it might have seemed — was okay with her.

I also talked things over with my friend and companion at the time, and she was just as filled with despair as I was. She'd been standing in a line at the bank in Harvard Square, listening in to the conversation of two perfectly nice middle-aged women in front of her. "Those kids at Kent State got exactly what they deserved," one woman said, and the other emphatically agreed with her. If that was America, we wanted out of it. We emigrated to Canada in the summer of 1970. I wish now that Canada was the country that I thought it was when I first crossed the border and saw the maple leaf flying.

AFTER I GOT MY bearings in a new country, I began to write again. I had brought with me over a thousand pages of stuff — musings, essays, poetry, random fragments — stories I'd finished, stories I'd abandoned, and notes for future stories, but I was also carrying around in my psyche the germ of a book that hadn't revealed itself yet.

It was going to be about a girl who should have been a boy and a boy who should have been a girl — that's all I knew — and I would write it for *my* community, whatever that was — if I actually had a community.

I wrote *Two Strand River* in the summer of 1975, opened with Leslie, my tomboy warrior girl, walking deserted streets and thinking about death. A retired competitive swimmer, she still swims every morning, and she's on her way to the pool, walking in the reflective gray quiet of Vancouver just before dawn, just on the edge of rain. She still has the keys to the high school where she used to train, and she swims there alone.

> She sank down into the starting position.
> Tense. Her entire body was holding. . . . tense,
> tense. She was carefully aware of her toes
> gripping the concrete. And then the second
> hand was at twelve and she was gone, released,
> shot forward and stretched into the racing dive.
> And for a moment, a particle of time so short
> she almost missed it, as she hung there drawn
> out over the water, fast, unbelievably fast, her
> reflection was racing up to meet her.

Her reflection on the other side of the mirror is Alan, the latest version of the feminine boys I'd been creating since I'd begun writing stories. He too is caught in a moment of quiet consciousness, staring into the mirror in his beauty shop, trying to really *see* himself.

He's appalled by the clarity of the mirror, seeing the minute tracery of blood vessels in the whites of his eyes, the dark rings around each cornea, the pores in his face.

But how easy to forget, become a caricature
of himself, in memory a blank oval, anything
but human with pores and blood vessels. And
could he stare into the mirror long enough to
see himself? But (and this was most important)
if he saw himself finally, would he remember?

Having opened by placing my characters in the eerie quiet of this self-reflective dawn, I simply kept on going. I didn't yet have much of a plot, but I planned to find that out as I went. I kept waiting to hit the usual blockages I'd always experienced in my writing, but there didn't seem to be any. Then, within days, my characters jumped up into full-blown reality and took over, and I realized that I'd lost any conscious control of the book. I didn't feel like the author. I felt like somebody taking dictation.

It was the closest thing to automatic writing I've ever done. My problem was not figuring out what was going to happen next; my problem was trying to keep up with what was already happening. I worked every day from eight-thirty in the morning to four in the afternoon and left the typewriter exhausted. And then, as I lay around in the evening trying to recover, my characters wouldn't let me alone but kept on talking to me. I fell asleep with them talking to me, and I woke up with them talking to me. I gave up any pretence of knowing where the book was going or what it was about. Every morning I thought, "What are those crazy people going to do today?"

I would say now was that I must have tapped into a hidden source deep in my psyche, that I was telling a version of a story that I had been carrying around for years. The first draft of *Two Strand River* took me only six weeks. I knew even at the time that the book was excessive, over the top, even melodramatic, simply crammed with too much stuff, that it badly needed an edit, but I hadn't yet learned how to edit my own work. That original draft, with only minor revisions, was exactly what was published by Press Porcépic in 1976.

When I held a copy of the finished book in my hands, I felt a sense of wonderment and completion that's hard to describe. If there's a character arc here, this is it: the little kid who had learned to tell stories by drawing cartoons on the tiles on the bathroom walls had grown up to become a novelist. I'd also fulfilled a promise I'd made to myself. In my strange recurring memory in which nothing happens, in the rainy blue twilight, caught in a self-reflective pause between day and night, between childhood and adolescence, I'd known that there had to be a story somewhere that I'd always wanted to read. Now I'd written it.

I'd suspected that my cross-gender protagonists would disturb some people, but I wasn't prepared for just how disturbed they were. The first reviewer chosen by *Books in Canada* sent the book back to the editor with words to the effect of, "I simply don't know what to say about it," and most of those who did review the book had never seen anything like it — and said so — but it acquired a cult following over the years, came to be labeled "a classic of Canadian magic realism," and was reprinted twice. When the HarperCollins edition was republished in 1996, Kirkus Reviews called *Two Strand River* "one of the best gender-bending novels now in print."

The reviewers who had commented on the gender of my two main characters had usually seen them as "transsexual" — to use the term that was current at the time — but if you study the text carefully, you will see that they're not. They're nonbinary just like their author.

# EPILOGUE

1

THE MOVEMENT KEPT ON GOING without me — campus protests, an alarming number of things blowing up, and in the spring of 1971 another huge march on Washington. In '72 Nixon bombed North Vietnam even more vigorously than Johnson had, but in '73 the Americans scrapped their Selective Service Act and signed the Paris Peace Accords. Watergate came in '74, the fall of Saigon in '75, and I was glad to be watching all of this from the northern side of the border. If you were a middle-class white guy, Canada was a fine place to live — peaceful, like a North American Switzerland — and I mistakenly thought that I was free from the terrible weight of American karma.

Just as I had imagined it would, the Women's Movement survived the '60s and flourished. The classic works of what we now call the Second Wave were written and published, and I read them for a while, but those women, for all the good points they were making, were not talking to me — they were organizing in their own community — and eventually I lost interest in eavesdropping on their conversations. There was also an element in some of that writing — not all of it — that I couldn't identify, but it put me off. Looking back, I see it now as transmisogyny.

So what happened to my particular circle of burnt-out friends and comrades from the American New Left? Hungry for meaning, some were attracted to huge narratives that explained everything — charismatic Christianity, Scientology, imported Tibetan Buddhism. Others found small progressive corners of the world where they could build careers. A few simply vanished, and to this day I don't know what happened to them. A bitter line of advice was circulating in those days — "You want to organize something? Start with your own life." Many of us did exactly that.

I organized my life primarily around writing novels. After *Two Strand River* was published, I was active in the literary scene, both the larger Canadian one and the local Vancouver one. I worked at a few more odd jobs, got some help from the Canada Council which made my life a hell of a lot easier. As the turbulence of the '70s and '80s gradually morphed into the becalmed '90s, my fifth novel was published, I got married, my daughter Liz was born, and I was hired to teach Creative Writing at the university level, the perfect job for me — I did what I taught and taught what I did. I had learned how to write fiction on my own, and it had taken me years to get anywhere. I wanted to make everything I had learned available to my students so that it wouldn't take them years to get anywhere.

MY GRANDMOTHER DIED in 1983. *It's a great life if you don't weaken.* I heard her say that countless times, and she believed it absolutely. If you weakened, life rolled over you and squashed you flat and destroyed you, so you had to maintain your firmness and your strength and your unshakable knowledge of what was right and what was wrong. She lived to be ninety-eight and never did weaken. As she was nearing the end of her life, she was struck by a grinding pain in her guts so severe that she cried out in the night. My mother sweet-talked their family doctor into making a house call. Hearing that the doctor was coming, my grandmother got up and got dressed, met the doctor in the living room, and chatted as though it were a social visit. "Tell the doctor about your pain," my mother said.

"What pain?" my grandmother said.

My mother died in 2005 at nearly ninety-four. In her last years she had dementia. She always knew who we were, but she had hardly anything to say, and it became increasingly difficult for me to connect the silent old person in front of me with the mother I used to know. For what turned out to be her last Christmas she stayed with us for a few days in a B and B near her care home. She could see a distant flicker of water through the window; it was a lake, but she took it for the Ohio River and said, "West Virginia."

No matter my own beliefs, I try to honor other people's. When my mother was dying, I asked for help from the hospital chaplain. He reminded her of what she'd said to me when we'd viewed my aunt Eleanor's body in the funeral home: "She's not there anymore. That's only her body. She's gone to be with God." He asked her if she still believed that, and she said that she did. They prayed together. The last thing I heard her say was, "I'm tired. I want to lie down."

My mother and grandmother gave me a great start in life. We didn't always see eye to eye — particularly during my stormy adolescence — but they did just fine. When I read Sartre's opinion on growing up fatherless — that it was a good thing because if he'd had a father, he would have been instantly absorbed into the patriarchy — I thought, you know, he's got a point.

I HAD SPENT the first half of my life in opposition to the dominant political ideology, and now it looked as though I was going to spend the second half that way too. The university, sheltering, as it does, oddballs of all types, seemed like a sanctuary to me, and in Creative Writing I tried to create a sanctuary inside a sanctuary, a safe and

nurturing place for my students to do the most important work in the world — figure out what they had to say
and how to say it. I had developed a pretty good sense of
what would sell, and if my students wanted to hear about
that, I was delighted to tell them, but I also abandoned
any preconceived notions I'd had about what "good"
writing should be. Instead I tried to see in my students'
work what was latent, what was emerging — what their
writing was trying to become — and help them to get it
there. To keep up with them, I had to read what they
were reading, share their enthusiasms, try to see their
visions. I learned as much from them, or more, as they
learned from me.

As wildly improbable as it seemed, I eventually
found myself happily married, living a quiet life in a
nice home with my wife and two daughters — and I liked
using those bland, colorless, uninformative words to tell
my own story. I *wanted* my life to be happy, quiet, and
nice — so that I could write fiction that was anguished,
clamorous, and subversive — but my life never stopped
feeling strange to me. I'd learned protective coloration
in military school; then I'd had years of practice in presenting as an ordinary heterosexual man, and that's the
way most people outside of my family saw me. I didn't
feel any need to correct that public image of myself. I
wasn't hiding, but I wasn't advertising my differences
either. I thought that my private life was nobody's business, and if anyone wanted to know what I was thinking,
they could read my novels.

My life had been focused on writing, teaching, and my family, but I began to feel the need to see what had been happening while I'd been gone, and plenty had been happening. Feminism had developed a Third Wave; some said that it began with the Riot Grrrl movement in the early 1990s when girls had formed their own bands, written and published their thoughts in zines. In *The Riot Grrrl Manifesto* Kathleen Hanna wrote that "girls constitute a revolutionary soul force that can, and will change the world for real." I couldn't have agreed with her more.

I read Eve Kosofsky Sedgwick's thorough analysis of the way feminine boys are attacked and undermined by theorists of all stripes. I read Julia Serano's wry comment on her transition: "The hardest part has been learning how to take myself seriously when the entire world is constantly telling me that femininity is always inferior to masculinity." In my twenties I'd had several encounters with psychiatrists — the certified kind with MDs after their names — and I'd come to the conclusion that when it came to the stuff that was bothering me, they didn't know anything whatsoever. If I'd been misguided enough to go to a psychiatrist later in life, at any time between 1994 and 2013 when *The Diagnostic and Statistical Manual of Mental Disorders IV* was in use, I would have been diagnosed with "gender identity disorder." I read in Judith Butler's *Undoing Gender* that such a diagnosis "seeks to uphold the gender norms of the world as it is currently constituted and tends to pathologize any effort to produce gender in ways that fail to conform to existing norms."

IF THE WORLD WERE to be bisected with one of those hypothetical lines in the sand, straight people on one side and non-straight people on the other, I would be on the non-straight side, and I'd known that all of my adult life. Although the claim has been challenged lately, gender identity has usually been considered to be, as psychologists put it, "stable across the lifespan," and mine certainly has been. When I look deep inside myself, I see that my gender in my seventies is exactly the same as it was in my earliest memories, but what has changed is the label I put on it. The best I could do as a kid was "like a girl," but under the binary that was not an admissible category for a gender. In the '60s I'd learned to call myself "androgynous," but that soon wore out its usefulness; an androgyny that was available to anyone, that could be chosen and cultivated, was not a gender either. I'd watched as the non-straight side kept adding letters to the list, going from GL to LGB to LBGTQ and so on, and I appreciated the attempts at inclusivity, but I was afraid that until they added K for Keith, I wouldn't be part of the team — that was how far beyond definition I felt myself to be.

I first saw the term "genderfluid" on the net sometime in 2009. The notion of gender fluidity as a descriptive metaphor had been around for a long time, and I had even used it myself, but what caught my attention was a new usage of the term. It now appeared to be referring to a specific gender identity, one just as legitimate as male or female. Hey, I thought, *genderfluid as a gender?* That was pretty good. Then, sometime later, I found another term beginning to appear — "nonbinary." That seemed to be a broad term for all those people who don't fit into the two-gender schema, and that was even better.

On Tumblr I found young trans people organizing in their own community and watched as their thinking evolved. The term "paradigm shift" has been overused to the point that it has lost much of its original impact, but there has been a genuine paradigm shift in the past decade: a narrative about gender in which I could not locate myself has been replaced by one in which I can. As a child or adolescent, or even well into young adulthood, I would probably have adopted one of the gender subcategories that the kids on Tumblr are creating, but I'm an old guy now, and I would say, simply, that I'm nonbinary.

When I believed that there was no one else like me, I thought that I must be doomed and damaged, possibly not even human. Now I know that there are many people who are like me, and that we are whole and perfect and will not be erased. Finding the right names for ourselves enables us to recognize each other. We are here now, we have always been here, and we will continue to be here as long as there are people on the planet.

# ACKNOWLEDGMENTS

*The Bridge* and *Fatherless* (West Virginia University Press, 2019) are meant to be entirely independent works, but given that they both cover some of the same events, a certain overlap in subject matter was inevitable. I have carefully avoided any actual duplication of writing, but both books contain edited excerpts from the interview that I conducted with my mother when she was in her eighties. The unedited transcript of the original interview from which both versions were taken is included in my literary papers, and I hold copyright on it.

Chapters 1 and 3 of "The Movement" include some writing that originally appeared in "The Author's Afterword" to my novel, *Looking Good* (Brindle & Glass, 2006). Chapter 5 of "The Movement" includes some writing that originally appeared in "The Afterword" to the HarperCollins edition of my novel, *Two Strand River* (1996), as well as text from the novel itself (Press Porcépic, 1976). I hold copyright on all of this material.

To protect the privacy of those who could still be living, I have changed the names of my childhood neighbors and classmates. All other persons in this book have their real names, with the exception of "let's call him Karl" from Chapter 4 of the "The Movement."

Andrea Bennett read the manuscript of *The Bridge* in an earlier version and offered invaluable editorial input. I took most of their suggestions, and the book is much the better for it. Thank you, Andrea. Also I must once again thank my most reliable critic, my wife, Mary; my sage and tireless agent, John Pearce; and Kelsey Attard and the entire Freehand team who have continued to support my work and have done such a great job in bringing *The Bridge* into the world. Finally, I want to thank my editor at Freehand, Deborah Willis. She has a superbly keen eye for rough edges, and she always knew what I was up to even when I didn't. Working with her was a joy.

I wrote this book while I was an uninvited but grateful guest on the unceded territory of the Squamish and Tsleil-Waututh Nations.

KEITH MAILLARD

*May 14, 2020*

KEITH MAILLARD is the author of fourteen novels, one book of poetry, and two memoirs. Twelve of his titles have been shortlisted for or won literary prizes. *Light in the Company of Women* was a runner-up for the Ethel Wilson Fiction Prize; *Motet* won that prize. *Hazard Zones* was short-listed for the Commonwealth Literary Prize, and *Gloria* was a finalist for the Governor General's Award. *Dementia Americana* won the Gerald Lampert Award for best first book of poetry in Canada. *The Clarinet Polka* was awarded the Creative Arts Prize by the Polish American Historical Association. Of his quartet, *Difficulty at the Beginning*, the first three volumes — *Running, Morgantown,* and *Lyndon Johnson and the Majorettes* — were shortlisted for the Weatherford Award while the quartet's final book, *Looking Good*, was longlisted for the Relit Award. His novel *Twin Studies* was awarded the 2019 Alberta Book of the Year Award in the fiction category.

Throughout his long career Maillard has published nonfiction essays and articles in newspapers, journals, and anthologies. In 2018 he contributed to *Refuse: Canlit in Ruins*, edited by Julie Rak, Hannah McGregor, and Erin Wunker. *The Bridge* is his second book-length work of creative nonfiction.

Maillard has taught in the Creative Writing Program at the University of British Columbia for over thirty years. He lives in Vancouver with his wife, author and editor Mary Maillard. For further information on Keith, including a complete publication list, please visit his website: keithmaillard.com